BUILDING A WEBSITE USING A CONTENT MANAGEMENT SYSTEM in 90 MINUTES

For a complete list of Management Books 2000 titles,
visit our web-site on http://www.mb2000.com

> The original idea for the 'In Ninety Minutes' series was presented to the publishers by Graham Willmott, author of 'Forget Debt in Ninety Minutes'. Thanks are due to him for suggesting what has become a major series to help business people, entrepreneurs, managers, supervisors and others to greatly improve their personal performance, after just a short period of study.

Titles in the original 'in Ninety Minutes' series include:

Forget Debt in 90 Minutes, Understand Accounts in 90 Minutes
Working Together in 90 Minutes, Supply Chain in 90 Minutes
Practical Negotiating in 90 Minutes, Faster Promotion in 90 Minutes
Find That Job in 90 Minutes, Become a Meeting Anarchist in 90 Minutes
Telling People in 90 Minutes, Strengths Coaching in 90 Minutes
Perfect CVs in 90 Minutes, Networking in 90 Minutes
Payroll in 90 Minutes, 25 Management Techniques in 90 Minutes
Budgeting in 90 Minutes, Active Learning in 90 Minutes

The series editor is James Alexander

> This new series of IT-focused 'in 90 Minutes' books will help readers travel through the sometimes confusing and esoteric world of Information Technology with greater ease and comprehension. The publishers acknowledge the help and guidance given by Martin Bailey, the author of this volume, in setting a great standard for the new series.

Titles in the 'IT in Ninety Minutes' series include:

Get More Visitors to Your Website in 90 Minutes
Building a Website Using a CMS in 90 Minutes
Think You Want a Website? in 90 Minutes
   ... others will be added as the series progresses

Submissions of possible titles for this series or for management books in general will be welcome. MB2000 are always keen to discuss possible new works that might be added to their extensive list of books for people who mean business.

BUILDING a WEBSITE USING a CMS in 90 Minutes

A guide to developing feature-rich websites with CMS systems such as Joomla! and Mambo

Martin Bailey

IIl.
2000

Copyright © Martin Bailey 2006

All rights reserved. No part of this publication may be reproduced, stored in a retrieval system, or transmitted in any form or by any means, electronic, mechanical, photocopying, recording, or otherwise without the prior permission of the publishers.

First published in 2006 by Management Books 2000 Ltd

Forge House, Limes Road

Kemble, Cirencester

Gloucestershire, GL7 6AD, UK

Tel: 0044 (0) 1285 771441

Fax: 0044 (0) 1285 771055

E-mail: info@mb2000.com

Web: www.mb2000.com

Printed and bound in Great Britain by 4edge Ltd of Hockley, Essex – www.4edge.co.uk

This book is sold subject to the condition that it shall not, by way of trade or otherwise, be lent, resold, hired out, or otherwise circulated without the publisher's prior consent in any form of binding or cover other than that in which it is published and without a similar condition including this condition being imposed upon the subsequent purchaser.

British Library Cataloguing in Publication Data is available

ISBN 1-85252-523-1 EAN 978-185252-523-1

Contents

Introduction		7
1.	What is a CMS?	9
2.	Evaluating a CMS System	17
3.	Installing your CMS	21
4.	Administration Section Overview	33
5.	Structuring Your Content	37
6.	Adding Content	43
7.	Security and Access Restrictions	55
8.	The Media Manager	59
9.	Installing Templates	63
10.	Making Your Own Joomla! Template	69
11.	Optimising Your Site for search Engines.	79
12.	Installing Additional Functionality	91
13.	Multi-lingual Sites	101
14.	Backing-up Your Site	109
Summary		117
Appendix 1 – CSS Styles List		119
Appendix 2 – Quick Guide to Installation and Configuration		121
Glossary		122
Index		125

Introduction

There are many free Content Management Systems (CMS) available. These 'web sites in a box' allow complex site structures to be up and running in a matter of hours using nothing but a web browser, with a variety of additional modules that deliver a comprehensive and functional site that would take months to write in-house from scratch. A CMS can be used from sites ranging from a basic personal site through to a large-scale e-commerce or content-driven site receiving millions of visitors.

While there are literally hundreds of open source CMS systems available empowering literally millions of sites – PHP-Nuke, PostNuke, Type3, Tikiwiki and Xoops to name but a few – Mambo and Joomla! are both respected and stable systems. As we will see, these two systems are almost identical. We will concentrate primarily on Joomla!, although you can evaluate any of the CMS out there and see what suits your needs. Although the content in this book discusses the Joomla! system in detail, the theory behind it will be virtually the same for any other system. All CMS are modular in their design, allow different templates to be applied and tweaked, and have a plethora of additional extensions available from third parties to add functionality. The concept of structuring content into sections and categories is also common across all CMS.

Why read this book?
Or, more to the point, why should you consider developing a CMS-powered site over one built from static HTML pages? As we'll cover in greater detail in the first chapter, there are many scenarios why you might install a CMS. *In short, once configured, a CMS will quickly deliver a slick, powerful site that is very easy to maintain – either by yourself or other people, and for little or no financial investment.*

In 90 minutes, readers will learn how to decide whether a CMS is suitable for their needs, identify the best CMS system for their needs, locate a suitable hosting company, upload the code and configure it to match their design and functionality needs.

1. What is a CMS?

As we covered in the introduction, CMS allow people with little or no computer experience to maintain and add content to web sites that can be very comprehensive in terms of both content and the functionality that it provides to its visitors (e.g. forums, e-commerce etc). A CMS consists of a frontend and backend – the frontend is the web site that users will see and the backend is where you administer the site.

What this means in plain English is that you can use a web browser to build a web site! All of your pages are split into sections and sub-categories, and various components can be plugged in to deliver additional functionality.

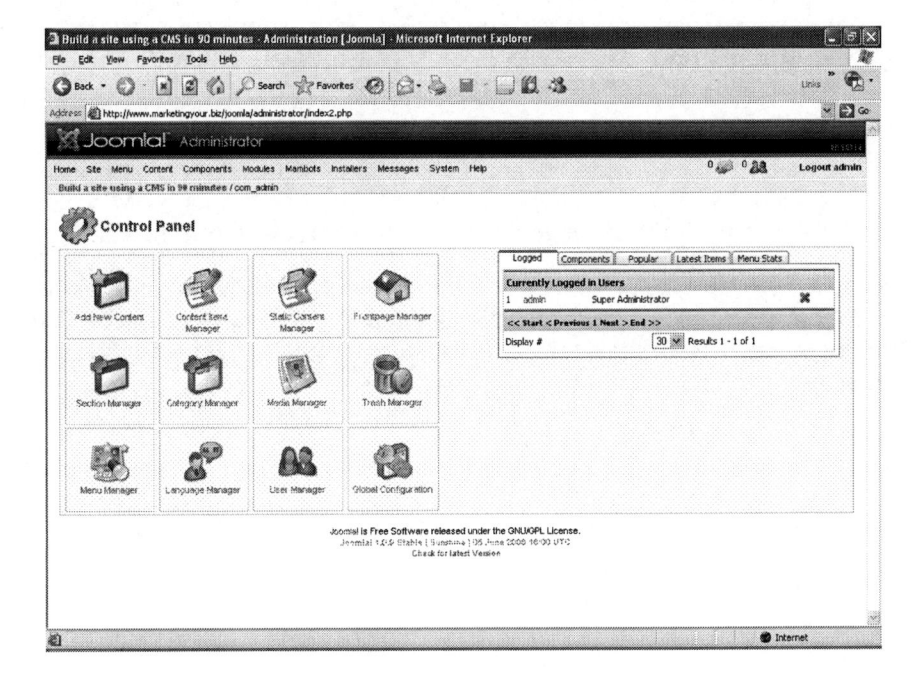

1.1. The backend of most CMSs provides a simple administrator interface to administer content.

Building a Website Using a CMS in 90 Minutes

All of the CMSs mentioned in the introduction are powered by two technologies – the PHP scripting language and the mySQL database system, which most Internet Service Providers (ISPs) support either with standard packages or for a nominal fee – normally around £100 per year.

Before we go into greater detail, we should clarify some terminology. There are several items you need to understand – components, modules and templates.

Components are effectively compete applications that can be plugged into the CMS. This might be a simple function such as a site map, or could be as comprehensive as a full e-commerce solution or forum.

Modules are usually associated with a specific component, and are 'boxes' of information that can usually be placed within the columns left or right of the main content window. For example, if you see a list of the top five news stories, latest items, a small calendar listing this month's events etc, these would be modules, some of which are linked to external components. Most CMSs will be supplied with some standard modules.

Templates are the designs that can be applied to the site. CMSs usually come with one or two templates installed. Popular CMSs normally have a plethora of free templates available. If you know a little HMTL and CSS, it is not difficult to customise these to meet your own needs.

Note: When you search for extra functionality on the CMS source site, this might be referred to as an extension, plugin or (confusingly) a module! The components/module terminology is used specifically with Mambo and Joomla! but differs when referring to other CMS systems.

What can a CMS system do?

Most CMSs will still have a far greater level of functionality 'out of the box' than the majority of 'static' HTML web sites out there. A static site is one that does nothing more than display the content that was originally written – it does not generally offer search functions and you will need to update other pages to link to new ones when they are written (e.g. if you write a new press release you'd need to go to your main press page and put a link to the newly created page).

A CMS is effectively a collection of hundreds (or even thousands) of pages of program scripts (PHP files) that read from and write to a database. Take the front page of any CMS-powered site: each time that page is loaded several 'queries' will be made to the database, such as:

What Is a CMS?

- Load the selected template (as your site might actually be able to be displayed using several different design templates)
- Decide which modules are to be displayed (such as main menu, user menu, banner advert, top five news, featured products, polls, who is online – the list of modules will depend on the functionality you have installed) and locate their relative positions within the template.
- Run queries relating to each module to see what has to be displayed – this might include:
  - list of items to appear in the menu, together with the links to relevant subsections/pages/components
  - selecting a random banner advert
  - displaying a calendar, with current events highlighted
  - displaying the most recent and/or most popular pages
- Select the content that is defined to be displayed within the main area of the site

And this is just for the front page of your site... As users navigate a CMS they use various plug-ins that can perform a wide range of tasks.

As the name suggests, a CMS is all about managing the content of your site. When content such as news gets older you can also place it in an archive. It's still available on the site, but moved into a more suitable location so that it doesn't clutter the current content.

Each CMS has varying degrees of community support, with individuals or companies developing either free or paid-for components and templates available for you to immediately download and plug into your site. Most of these are free, and those that are chargeable tend to be cheap (from £10 to £100).

Most CMSs will have some components built in or available that will deliver the following:

- Ability to create and categorise content into sections and subcategories e.g. a main section called Products, sub-categories for product ranges a, b and c, with each category then having individual product pages
- Auction systems – create your own Ebay!
- Banner adverts – sell advertising space, and track clickthrough rates
- Classified adverts – allow people to place free classified adverts, which is a great way to get repeat visitors to your site
- Discussion groups (forums) – build a community, allowing people to discuss topics defined by categories

- E-commerce – add a full shopping cart system to your site
- Fill-in-the-blank forms – for either a simple 'contact us' form through to complex surveys
- Frequently Asked Questions engine
- Games
- Glossary, with automatic highlighting of definitions on every page that terms appear on
- Multi-lingual support – built expansive sites in several languages
- Newsletter subscription and management
- Photo Gallery – easily upload and categorise large numbers of photos
- Polls/surveys – gauge and log visitors opinion
- RSS news feeds – display content dynamically from other sites
- Site map
- Search facility.

This is by no means a finite list, and the home development page for each CMS (for example www.joomla.org) usually has a 'Downloads' (often call projects, extensions or components) section detailing the various components available.

What does a CMS cost?

There are CMS available costing many thousands of pounds, however this book concentrates on those that are open source and (more importantly) free. Open source software is similar in idea to 'free software' but slightly less rigid than the free software movement. Users of open source software are also able to view the source code, alter and re-distribute open source software. There is, however, less of an emphasis in the open source movement on the right of information and source code to be free and, in some cases, companies are able to develop proprietary products based on open source ones. One such example is **Mambo**, developed by Miro International – an open source version is available as well as a more capable commercial version, which the company offers bespoke development for. Incidentally, PHP (the scripts that generate the final HTML code that you see) and mySQL (the database that stores your content) are also open source.

CMS vs HTML?

So, with all of these feature-rich CMSs out there, why should anyone write a HTML (or the newer XHTML standard) website anymore? If you have a very basic requirement, then a CMS is a sledgehammer to crack a walnut. They can also be semi-restrictive in the way that content can be laid out – most

What Is a CMS?

work on a two or three column layout. I say semi-restrictive, as if you have the skills you can design your own templates and move away from many of the 'samey' sites.

If you just want a way to easily manipulate your current HTML site without going back to your web designer, consider products such as Macromedia Contribute. The web designer maintains the look and feel of the site in Contribute's big brother – Dreamweaver, but allocates editable regions that other staff can access through Contribute. The designer then issues 'keys' for Contribute users, who can then use the software's built-in web browser to access pages on the site, clicking Edit to gain control over the content. Contribute works in a very similar way to a word processor, so if someone is reasonably familiar with Microsoft Word they will easily be able to master Contribute! Once done the user clicks 'Save and Update' and the web site is immediately updated. The web designer can then synchronise his copy with the live version to ensure no data is overwritten.

CMS sites are not without their problems. They are sometimes prone to security vulnerabilities, which may allow others to gain access to your administration section (and therefore your entire site's contents). Also, updating the core CMS to a newer version might cause older extensions to function erratically or not at all. This should not be seen as a 'show-stopper' though – just exercise caution when a new release of your chosen CMS becomes available, and visit the forums of it and the major extension you rely on. If no-one else is reporting problems (or you see fixes appear that solve any mentioned) then you should be safe to install. It is also worthwhile running a mirror test site somewhere, with a duplicate copy of your database and files – this way you can safely perform update and test without affecting your main site.

When should I consider a CMS?

Maybe you are just starting out with an idea for a site? Or perhaps you already have a HTML-powered site that you either want to add some functionality to or migrate completely over to a CMS? There's no reason why you can't install a CMS in a subfolder within an existing site, tweak it to mimic the existing design and then make use of some of the extended functionality the CMS provides. This would, however, not be using a CMS to its full potential, as you would not be able to take advantage of features such as the site search and sitemap – they would only cover the content within the CMS, and not your original site.

HTML-based site	CMS-powered site
• Allows for a much greater flexibility in design layout • Can possibly be better optimised for search engines • Relatively easy to build a basic site using today's WYSIWYG design tools • You have full control over the code behind your site, which may be important for the more technically competent user • Can be expensive if developed externally • Limited functionality • Adding other features generally requires separate modules that won't communicate with each other • Updating requires either web developing skills or special tools such as Macromedia Contribute	• There are many good free CMS available • Speed to market - you can have the basic shell of your site live minutes after uploading the files by ftp • Low-risk - easy to test-drive a CMS on suitable web space, also available very cheaply • Very easy to maintain using only a web browser - administer your site anywhere in the world • Wide range of extensions to add further features and functionality • Can be restrictive in terms of layout in comparison to more flamboyant HTML sites • You have limited control over outputted code • Some CMS do not generate fully W3C compliant code (although this is rapidly changing) • Like your Operating System, there can be some security risks that may allow others to gain administrator access to your site • Upgrades to core CMS code may create problems in installed extensions

When NOT to use a CMS

If you already have a basic HTML site and just need one additional feature, such as e-commerce, then a CMS may not be the best tool. There are plenty of great e-commerce tools (such as Actinic or PayPal) that will either build you a complete shopping site or integrate with your existing pages. Perhaps you want to add a discussion group to your site – again, there are plenty of cheap/free scripts that will provide this functionality. So the question is how you plan to develop your site in the future? Adding separate elements means just that – they are separate. There will be no integration or interaction between them. Think of your site's long-term goal – if a function such as e-commerce is the main goal, then you should evaluate relevant shopping systems, which often have some additional features that might cover your needs. One excellent open source e-commerce system is OsCommerce, which also has some integration with several CMS so that they can share a common user database. Visit www.oscommerce.com for more information on this.

Summary

As we proceed through the book you will get a clearer idea of what a CMS can do for you, but for now you can see that for little or no financial investment, and with minimal technical knowledge you can get a highly functional site live in a very short timeframe. Once live, this site can be easily maintained from any PC connected to the Internet. The end result is a much quicker return on investment, quicker speed to market and the ability for more people to administer the site from anywhere in the world.

2. Evaluating a CMS System

No doubt you have already reached the conclusion that you need a CMS system, but which one do you use? We mentioned some of the flamboyantly named systems earlier. Each one has their own web site that has a thriving community of developers within its forums, so you could trawl through each one until you find what you are looking for. There is a much easier way: www.opensourcecms.com. This site takes all of the known open source CMS systems that run on mySQL and PHP and provides trial versions for you to play with. Every two hours the server reboots and installs fresh copies of each CMS, so you really do get to play around with a 'virgin' installation. They publish a link to the frontend, with an administration username/ password to allow you access to the backend as well.

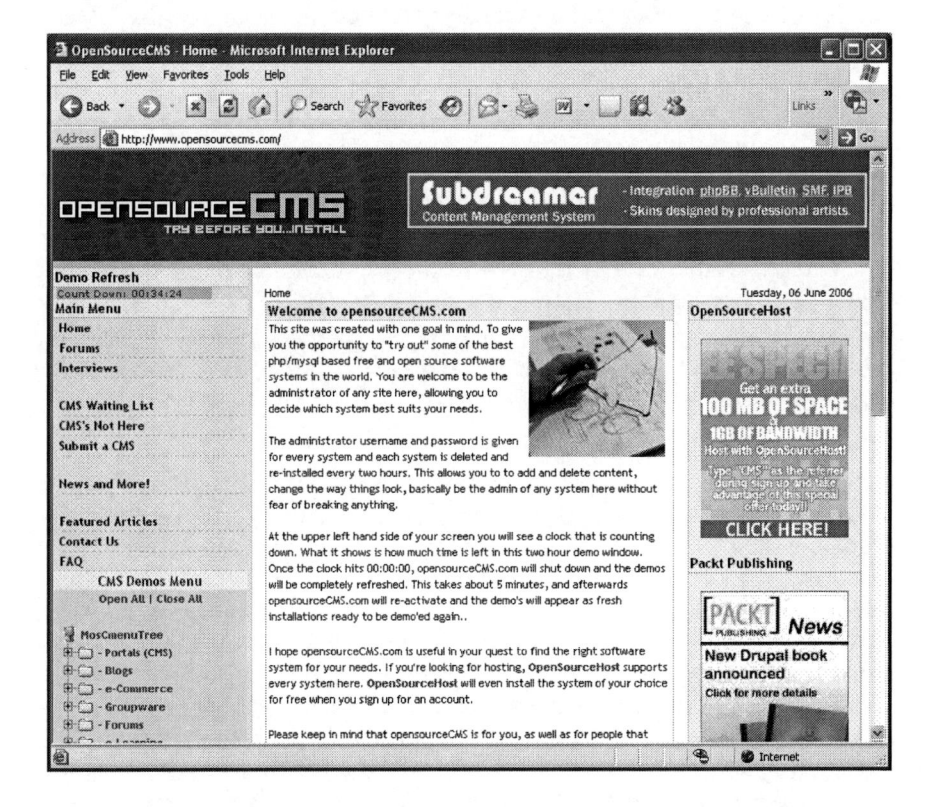

2.1. Opensourcecms.com should be your first port of call.

Once you are at the site you will see a tree menu on the left-hand side. We are interested in the 'Portals (CMS)' menu option, although you may want to familiarise yourself with some of the other systems available (e-commerce only, groupware, forums, galleries etc) as perhaps one day you will have a standalone project that does not require a full CMS but can benefit from one of these systems.

At the time of writing there are around 40 CMS systems listed within the Portals (CMS) section. Clicking on each one will give you the official description from the developers, a link to their site and then links to frontend and backend sections hosted on opensourcecms.com. Underneath here is where the really valuable information is – the user comments. While you should not take everything you read here as gospel, if every single user comment cites bugs, slow development, security issues, slow operation and complex to use then you know its time to move onto the next one. This is the first litmus test that you can do to get a feel for how well the CMS is performing from a users' perspective.

Incidentally, it is worth noting that opensourcecms.com runs on the Mambo CMS...

The purpose of this book is to help you to select a system that can provide a fully functional alternative to a static HTML site. It needs to allow content to be easily added and should have the ability to easily plug in additional functionality – either from already-developed components or for you to write custom-built applications. That limits us to either the Portals (CMS) section or perhaps also the CMS Lite section, which focuses on more lightweight systems – these may be more suited to simple information sites that do not require some of the additional functions a full CMS can offer.

Why Mambo/Joomla!?

Out of all of the systems listed on opensourcecms.com, I could have chosen several systems that are outstanding. The reason I selected (initially) **Mambo** is that (a) it is very easy to set up, (b) it is very easy to use, (c) it is very easy to customise, (d) it has a good security track record and (e) there is a very large community of developers supporting it. **Joomla!** is actually a 'fork' of Mambo – in August 2005 the chief developers of Mambo had a parting of the ways from Miro International (mentioned in Chapter 1). As the source code was open source they simply started the Joomla! system from where they left off with Mambo. While at the time of writing both systems are still compatible with each other, it is almost inevitable that components that used to work with both will fall into one camp or another – already developers of such components are tying their colours to one or other mast.

Evaluating a CMS system

Either way both systems will probably still be successful – Mambo has a huge existing base of developers and Joomla! already has a loyal following. Currently there is very little difference to the untrained eye (apart from a slightly different style of icons in the backend menu), so for the purpose of conformity we are selecting Joomla! as our chosen CMS from hereon in.

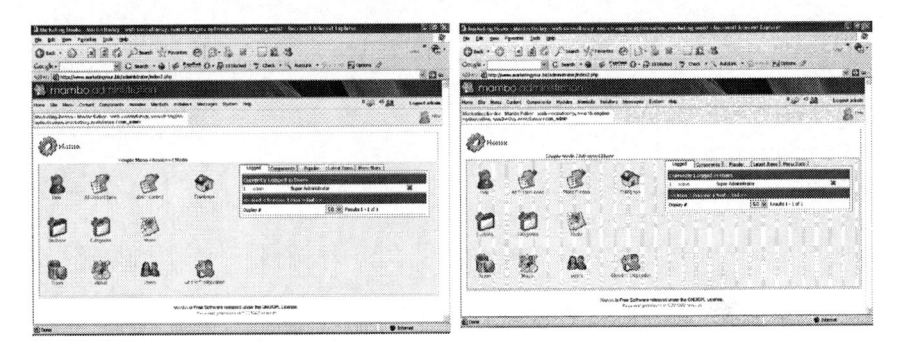

2.2. Spot the difference – the Joomla! And Mambo backends look almost identical.

Summary

You have plenty of choice when it comes to selecting a CMS, and while the rest of this book predominantly features Joomla!, do not take it as read that this is the best system available. It is good, but perhaps there is another system that more specifically meets your needs. Test the different systems available on opensourcecms.com before you decide. Also consider the functions (such as forums, e-commerce etc) that you are going to need, and ensure that the relevant extensions are available and well-supported/developed.

3. Installing Your CMS

Now that we have selected our chosen CMS, the next stage is to get it live. While there are various ways that you could bring this system online, we are going to focus on the easiest and most cost-effective method – to buy low-cost hosting services from an ISP rather than setting up your own server to run it on. If the latter is your preferred method, then this will no doubt be widely documented with your selected CMS.

So, back to selecting our ISP. This part is simple – you need an ISP that offers a Linux server, running the Apache web server and supporting PHP and mySQL – this configuration is known as L.A.M.P. (Linux, Apache, mySQL and PHP). The best way forward is to call the prospective ISP and simply ask if their web space will support the Mambo or Joomla! CMS systems. If they are not familiar with these then you could also mention PHP-Nuke, which is probably the most well known but also (allegedly!) notoriously insecure – if that works then Joomla! should. If they offer a 30-day money-back guarantee, then you are reasonably safe to go ahead.

How much space will you need?
This all depends on what you intend to store. If your site is text based then the content will be relatively small, but if you intend to add in graphics, movies, music files etc then the sky could be the limit. Joomla! itself will take up around 5MB, but this is not including the additional components and content you will no doubt install. Your content is stored in the mySQL database itself, which will probably not count as part of your web space. Most ISPs nowadays will give several thousand of MB of space, so this should be an issue only to larger projects.

You should also consider bandwidth requirements. A busy site, especially a graphics-heavy one, will drain your allotted bandwidth, so shop around for an ISP offering overly generous traffic amounts.

One such ISP in the UK is Heart Internet (www.heartinternet.co.uk). For around £130 they offer unlimited web space and bandwidth. They have many Joomla! sites running on their servers, some of which are mine, and I have never experienced problems during installation.

Installation

Step 1: Download Joomla!
The first step is to actually get the software you intend to install. Go to

Building a Website Using a CMS in 90 Minutes

Joomla.org and follow the download link to the latest version. You need to download the 'full package' of the latest version – the download section may list several upgrade packages or previous releases which can sometimes push the full and latest package download onto a second page. Download the ZIP file to your PC and decompress it to a folder. You should also download any installation documents available, as the installation procedure may have changed since this book was written. The process of unzipping can actually take several minutes as there are over 1600 files spanning 240 folders in the current Joomla! system. It is worth also downloading the Joomla! manual (available from the Help section of the Joomla! site) – while it is quite technical and does not go into much detail in certain areas, it may give you better depth in areas you are initially finding a little tricky.

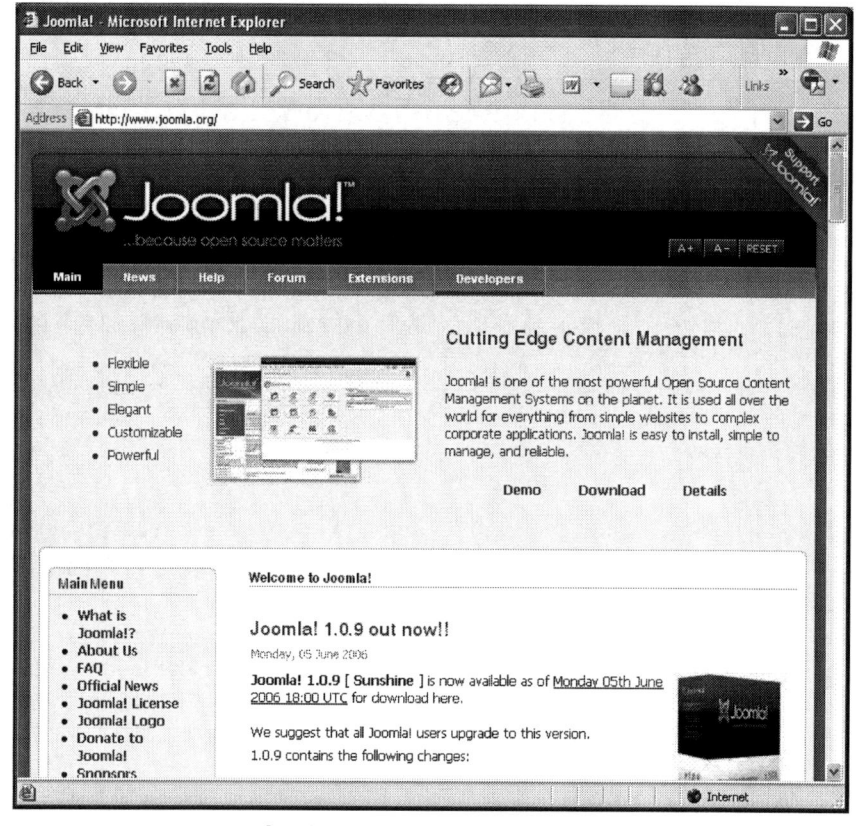

3.1. Getting the software is the easy bit!

Installing Your CMS

Step 2: Upload your source files
You will need two things – the FTP information for your web space and some FTP software. There are plenty of free program such as SmartFTP (www.smartftp.com) that will do the job. FTP is the method used to connect your PC to your web space.

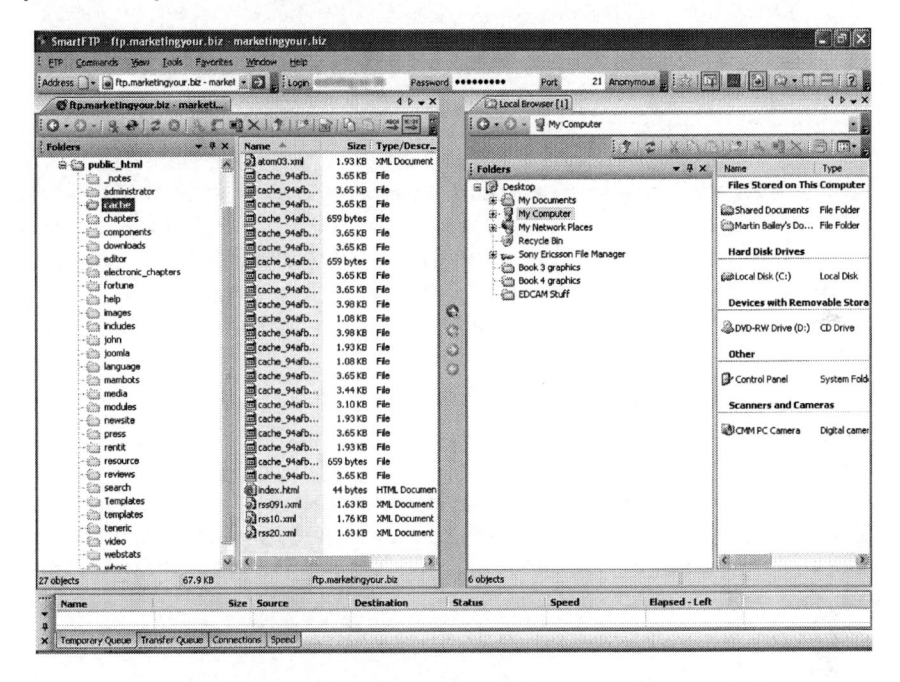

3.2 SmartFTP shows your hard drive in one window and your server's data in another.

You will need four pieces of information:

- the host name, which could be your domain name or an IP address
- your FTP username
- your FTP password
- whether your web site will reside in a sub-folder – sometimes when you 'ftp' into your space it will place you one directory higher than your web address will access, so you might have to open a directory called public_html, web or www (as shown in the previous screenshot).

On rare occasions you may have to enter a port number, but this is usually 21 which all FTP applications will default to.

Once you have established a connection between your computer and the server, locate where your decompressed Joomla! files are. How you upload these files will depend on your current site's status.

New sites
If you are creating a new site and there is no issue with anyone seeing the site as it is built then you can upload all of the files into the 'root' folder

Replacing an existing site
If you are upgrading a site to a CMS then you might not want it to go live straight away. Just create a sub-folder and upload your files to here. Once you are ready to go live you can simply move them to the root folder – you will also have to make a minor modification to the core configuration file (configuration.php) to point it at the new location. For more information on moving a CMS review the relevant forums, as there will be plenty of advice on this subject.

Step 3: Create your database
This process will differ depending on your ISP. Some ISPs will only give you access to one or a few databases, and will provide you with the database name, along with the username and password required to access it. Other ISPs will provide you with a backend control panel that allows you to create databases. If yours provides set database names, then you can move onto step 4. If not, go into your control panel and create your database and username/password. Make a note of these, ready for the next stage.

Installing Your CMS

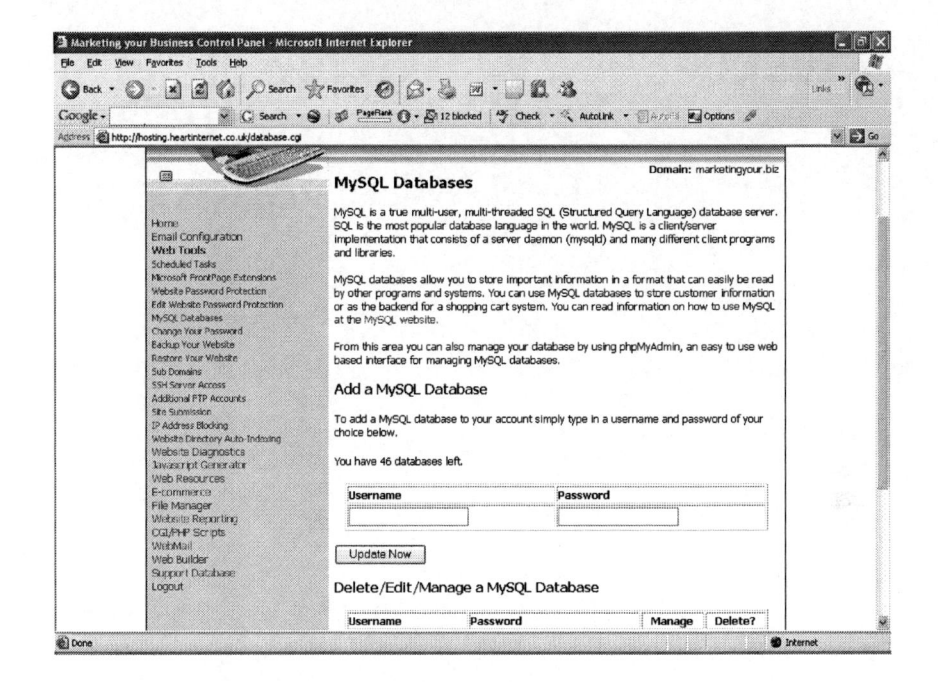

3.3. Some ISPs will provide a control panel where you can create your databases.

Step 4: Run the installation

Depending on your server this next stage will either be very easy or fraught with problems, however Joomla! has one of the most simple and intuitive installation procedures of any CMS available today. There are six screens for the installation procedure for Joomla. Open your web browser and type in your address (adding in the subfolder name if you did not upload to the root directory) – you will be greeted with the standard Joomla pre-installation check screen. A number of tests will be run on your server to check that the relevant services and permissions exist.

Building a Website Using a CMS in 90 Minutes

pre-installation check

Pre-installation check for:
Joomla! 1.0.9 Stable [Sunshine] 05 June 2006 16:00 UTC

If any of these items are highlighted in red then please take actions to correct them. Failure to do so could lead to your Joomla installation not functioning correctly.

PHP version >= 4.1.0	Yes
- zlib compression support	Available
- XML support	Available
- MySQL support	Available
configuration.php	Writeable
Session save path	Writeable
/tmp	

Recommended settings:

These settings are recommended for PHP in order to ensure full compatibility with Joomla. However, Joomla will still operate if your settings do not quite match the recommended

Directive	Recommended	Actual
Safe Mode:	OFF:	OFF
Display Errors:	ON:	ON
File Uploads:	ON:	ON
Magic Quotes GPC:	ON:	ON
Magic Quotes Runtime:	OFF:	OFF
Register Globals:	OFF:	OFF
Output Buffering:	OFF:	OFF
Session auto start:	OFF:	OFF

Directory and File Permissions:

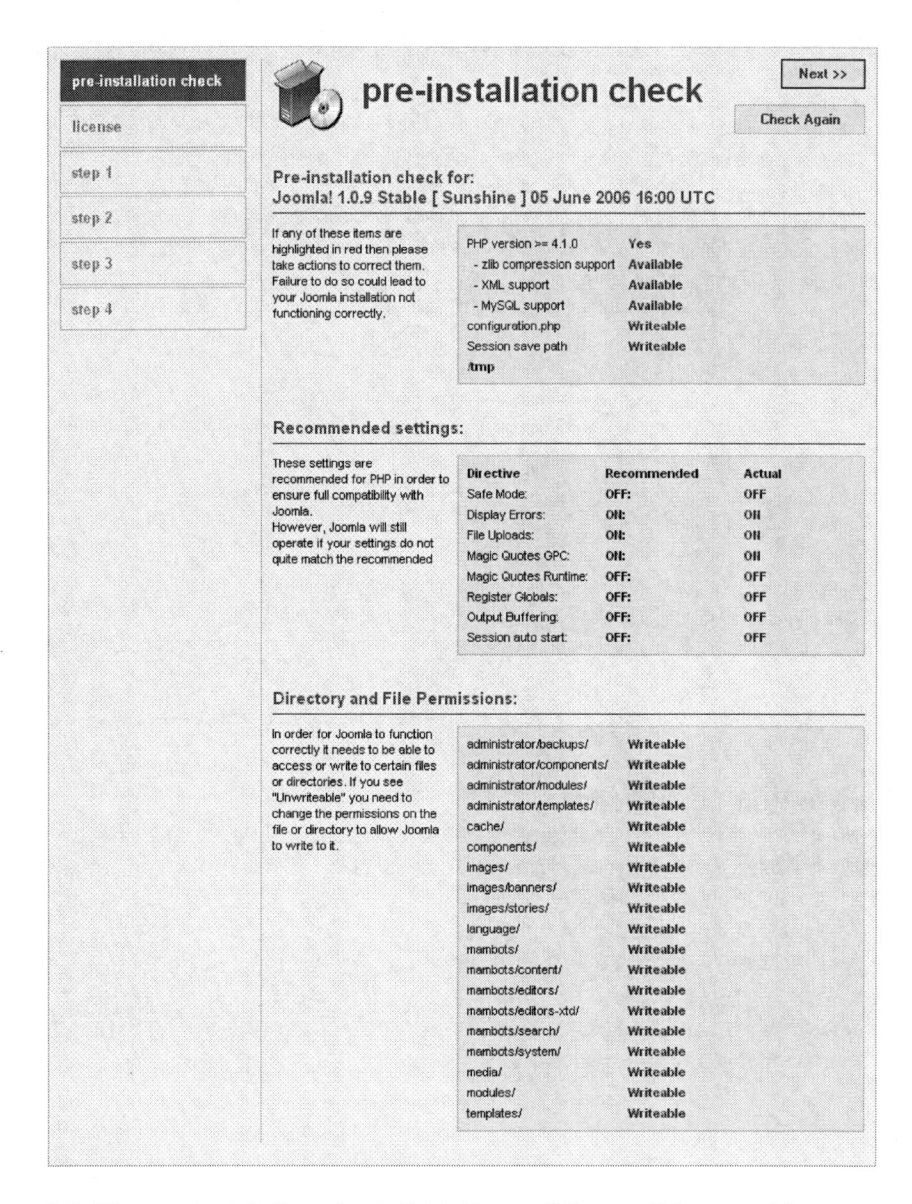

In order for Joomla to function correctly it needs to be able to access or write to certain files or directories. If you see "Unwriteable" you need to change the permissions on the file or directory to allow Joomla to write to it.

administrator/backups/	Writeable
administrator/components/	Writeable
administrator/modules/	Writeable
administrator/templates/	Writeable
cache/	Writeable
components/	Writeable
images/	Writeable
images/banners/	Writeable
images/stories/	Writeable
language/	Writeable
mambots/	Writeable
mambots/content/	Writeable
mambots/editors/	Writeable
mambots/editors-xtd/	Writeable
mambots/search/	Writeable
mambots/system/	Writeable
media/	Writeable
modules/	Writeable
templates/	Writeable

3.5. The pre-installation check list tells you if there will be a problem

If your server is correctly configured then all of the answers should be in green. The first range of items are critical to Joomla!'s functionality. If any of these items are in red then speak to your ISP. The second block, while still

Installing Your CMS

important should not stop Joomla! from running. The final block shows whether Joomla! can write to various directories. If they cannot be written to this can be easily fixed by changing the 'permissions' using a command within your FTP software known as 'CHMOD'.

If, for example, the cache folder was not writeable (and shown in red in the pre-installation check), perform the following:

- Open SmartFTP (or your chosen FTP software)
- Select the cache folder
- Find out how the CHMOD command is performed – this is usually done by right-clicking over the relevant file or folder, and selecting CHMOD or Properties
- From the resulting dialog box select 755 (or tick the check boxes until 755 appears), which denotes that the 'user' (or server) can write to the folder

Once you have CHMODed all required files/folders click on the Check Again icon, ensuring that all items are now green. Click on Next to continue. Now read and accept the GNU/GPL (General Public License) agreement, which is unlike most of the restrictive licenses that most software is supplied against.

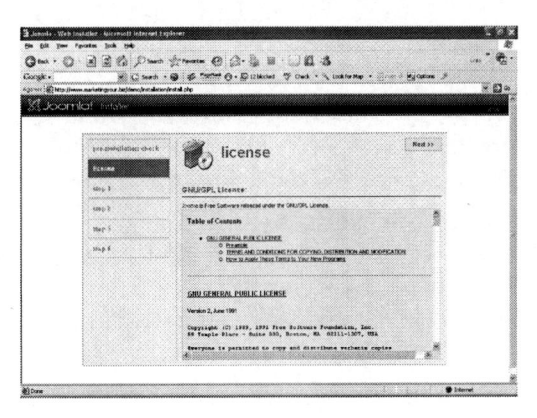

3.6. Agreeing to the GNU/GPL license is not difficult, as there are not many restrictions

On the next page you now need to enter the database information. There are four critical fields – hostname, mySQL username, password and database name.

Hostname is often set to localhost, although your ISP may advise you of a different setting – if so, use that. Next you can either enter the username, password and database that was supplied to you or that you created. You don't need to change the table prefix from 'jos_' unless you have another Joomla! installation and only have access to one database. If you are writing over an existing Joomla! installation then you can tick 'drop existing tables' to delete tables that will be overwritten by the new installation. Dropped tables can also be backed up by ticking the appropriate box. Lastly, you can install a sample set of data, which can be easily deleted once you get the hang of the system.

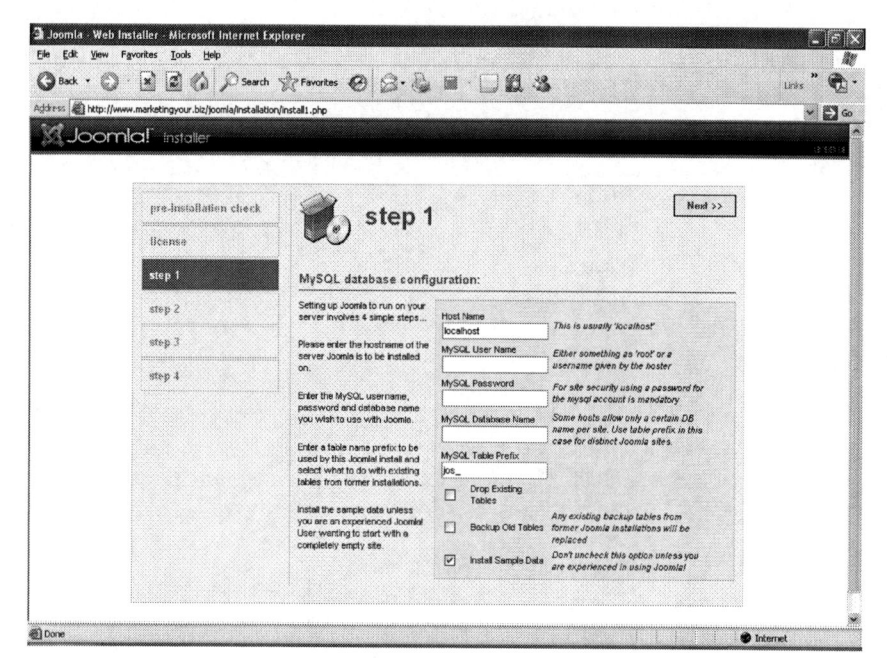

3.7. Make sure you enter the right database information!

Clicking on Next will run tests on the entered settings to ensure that Joomla! can communicate with your database. If it cannot, go back and check your settings again, talking with your ISP if necessary to verify settings. The most common mistakes are to enter the wrong host, username or database name – people generally get their passwords right!

Once Joomla! is talking to your database you can enter your site title. Note that this will also be used as a title to your emails, so ensure that it will be also relevant in that context.

Installing Your CMS

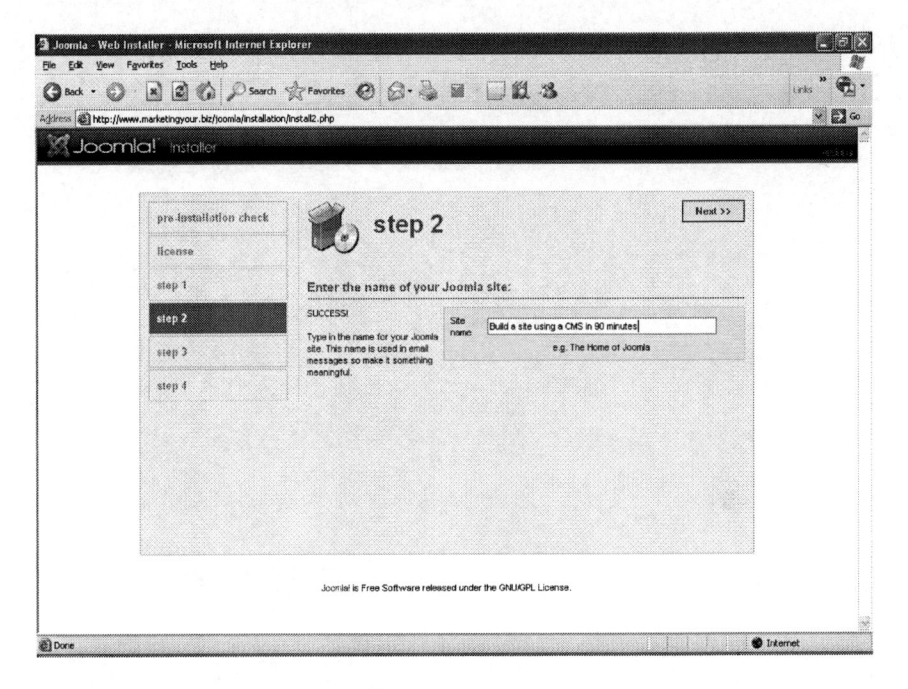

3.8 Enter a relevant title to your web site

If you've got this far you can see light at the end of the tunnel – the URL and server path to your Joomla! installation will be displayed, which you should not need to change unless this has been incorrectly detected (which is very rare). Enter your email address and admin password. Don't worry about the CHMOD options, as you can tighten security within the general configuration section later.

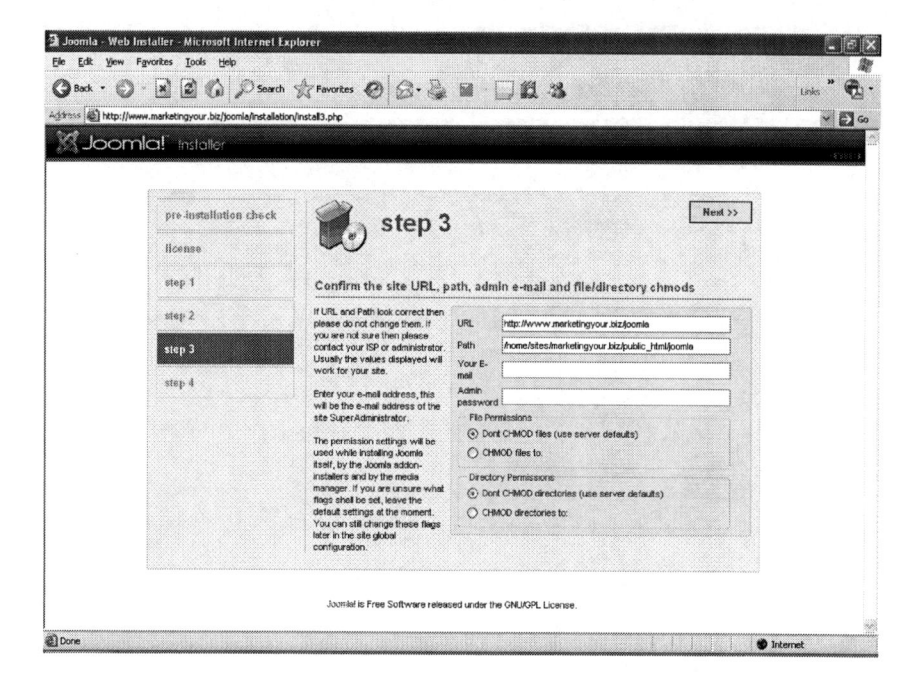

3.9. Check the details and enter your email and password

That's it! All of the areas that generally cause most problems are behind you now.

On the last screen you will see confirmation of the username and password needed to log into the site. There is one last task to perform before you can view your site – you need to delete the installation folder, so that nobody can repeat the above process and trash your site! Open your FTP software, connect to your web space, select the \installation folder and delete it. (Some FTP programs, such as WS_FTP_LE, require you to delete the files first and then the empty folders afterwards). Now you can view your virgin site.

Installing Your CMS

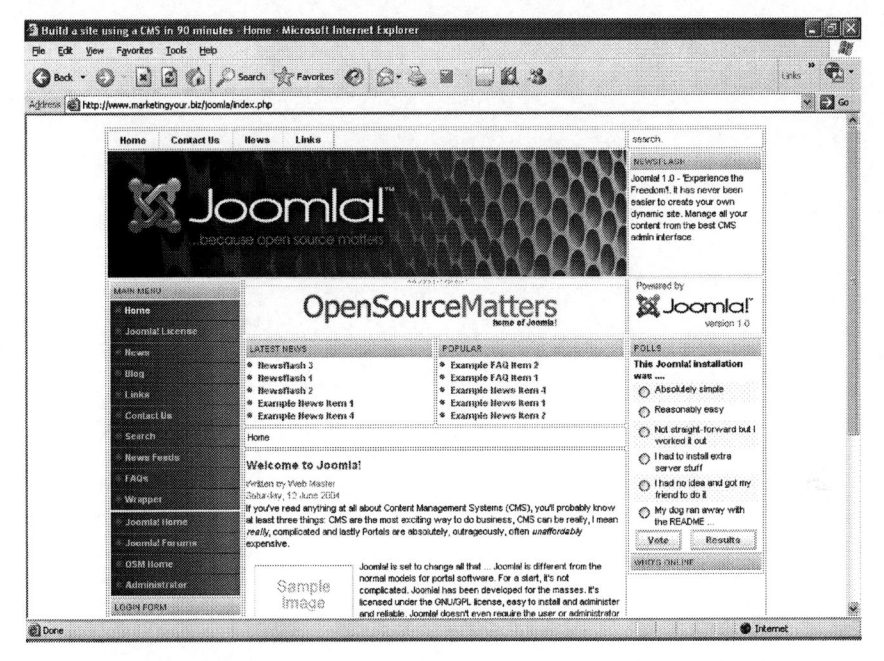

3.10. The standard front page after an installation with sample data

Summary

Generally the longest element of a Joomla! installation is the transferring of the core files themselves – if you have an ISP that is correctly configured for CMSs then installation can be done literally within 1-2 minutes once the files are on the server. Check with your ISP before you try to install a CMS to ensure that they actually support it. One ISP I came across in Italy not only didn't offer support for CMSs, but they actually refused to allow users the ability to even install them from their servers! (This was a Windows-based ISP, and while many CMS will run on Windows, the Linux OS and Apache web server is their preferred platform).

4. Administration Section Overview

On the last page of the installation process you were prompted with your username and a password to log into the back end administration section. Let's put that to use and go to www.yourdomain.com/administrator/ (not forgetting to modify the URL if you installed to a subfolder). Enter your details and you will be greeted with the screen that will provide total control over your web site.

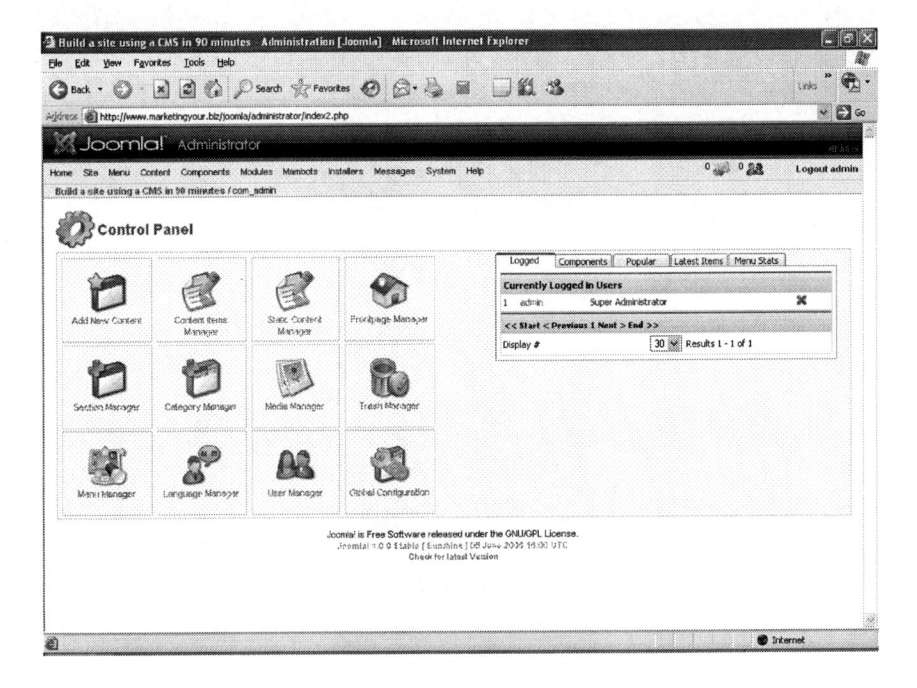

4.1 The Administration menu gives you complete access to your site's content

Joomla! provides various methods of getting to your content to edit it. First off are the twelve brightly coloured icons, which give access to the most frequently used functions, such as adding or amending content, editing content from the front page, managing media files, editing menus etc. On the right of the screen is a tabbed menu which gives swift access to information such as the number of logged in users, installed components, popular items, latest items and menu stats. Clicking on any of the items

Building a Website Using a CMS in 90 Minutes

within each tab takes you straight to an item – for example, clicking on Polls within Components will bring up the list of polls running, which you can then edit, or clicking on an item from the popular or latest items lists will bring up that content item for editing. Finally, at the top of the screen is a comprehensive drop-down menu that provides access to all items and functions. All-in-all, this is a simple interface and, if you can use Word or a web browser, you will feel right at home with Joomla! There is usually more than one way to access the information you want, and over time you will get to learn them all and choose a favourite method.

As the top menu covers all aspects of the system, let's run through each menu. We will only discuss what the menus hold, rather than each menu option at this stage:

Home:
   Straight link back to the main administration page.

Site:
   Provides access to fundamental aspects of your site, such as configuration, languages, media manager, previewing your site, statistics, template, trash (recycle bin) and user management.

Menu:
   Here you can modify the various menus that can be placed within Joomla! Some menus (such as Top) may not be used, depending on the template in use, so the main ones to remember are the 'main' and 'user' menus.

Content:
   This is where you create the structure of your site to place content into (through the section and category managers), and then edit it.

Components:
   Here you can modify the configuration, settings and content relating to functions (such as banners, polls and web links)

Modules:
   These are 'blocks' of functionality that are placed within various specified regions within your site, but outside of the main content area e.g. around the edges of your site. Each module can generally be configured to hide/display content, change position and use a different style sheet. This menu displays modules used in the front and back end.

Mambots:
This term is a legacy from Mambo that is still referred to with the same name within Joomla! Mambots are hidden elements of functionality. For example, if you install the popular VirtueMart shopping cart component you will also want to install the search mambot, which will scan any products within the shopping component when users perform a search anywhere else on the site. This menu option allows you to view, configure, enable or remove Mambots.

Installers:
A single menu that gives access to all of the installation screens, covering templates, components, language, modules and mambots.

Messages:
Allows the configuration of the private messaging system for use by administrators.

System:
Provides system and server information, as well as 'checking in' items that may have been inadvertently locked.

Help:
Links to Joomla's comprehensive help system, although this can be replaced with your own help page – useful if you are developing a site for someone else and want to build a custom help system for them.

Note: If others are likely to require back-end access you can set them a lower security level, which will hide some options such as Installers and Site menus – this will be covered later on.

Summary
The back end navigation system provides an 'application-style' interface which you will quickly get used to. All of the screens underneath these menus have common elements (such as the New, Edit and Save buttons), so once you learn how to perform one task all of the processes become easier.

5. Structuring Your Content

You now have one of the most powerful Content Management Systems running on your web space, although at the moment you have no content to manage! Adding structure to you content is about categorising it, not simply creating a page and linking it to a menu.

5.1. The main icons associated with content

Above are the main icons that you will use to create your structure, add in your content, upload images and quickly manage content that appears on your front page.

Before we delve into these in greater detail, we need to have a clearer understanding of how our content will be categorised.

Sections and categories explained
Joomla! allows two levels of categorisation – sections and categories within those section. For example you could create a section called Products, with three categories underneath named DVDs, Music CDs, and mobile phone ringtones. Subsequent pages are then allocated one of the three categories. Now imagine that you have three more sections, each with at least three sub-categories – that gives us twelve categories in which content can be placed.

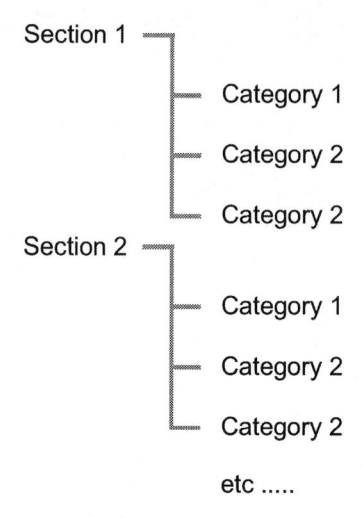

```
Section 1 ─┐
           ├── Category 1
           ├── Category 2
           └── Category 2
Section 2 ─┐
           ├── Category 1
           ├── Category 2
           └── Category 2

           etc .....
```

Before moving on, you should write down a list of the pages (or content types) that you intend to place on your site, then try to break them into sections and categories. It may be that you only have one section and one or two categories – that's fine, as you can easily create more and move content into them later. That is the beauty of Joomla!

Note: While all content (with the exception of static content, covered later) needs to be placed within sections and categories, you can link from the menus to a section, category or individual items. This is one of the most difficult elements for new Joomla! users to comprehend, so try to separate in your mind the categorising of content from the menus that link to it. Sections and categories can also be displayed in different ways, which we will also cover later. For now, concentrate on understanding how you will define and segregate your content.

Creating your sections

Either click on the Section Manager icon or click Content, then Section Manager on the menu. If you installed the sample data then you should have the following screen, with three sections created:

Structuring Your Content

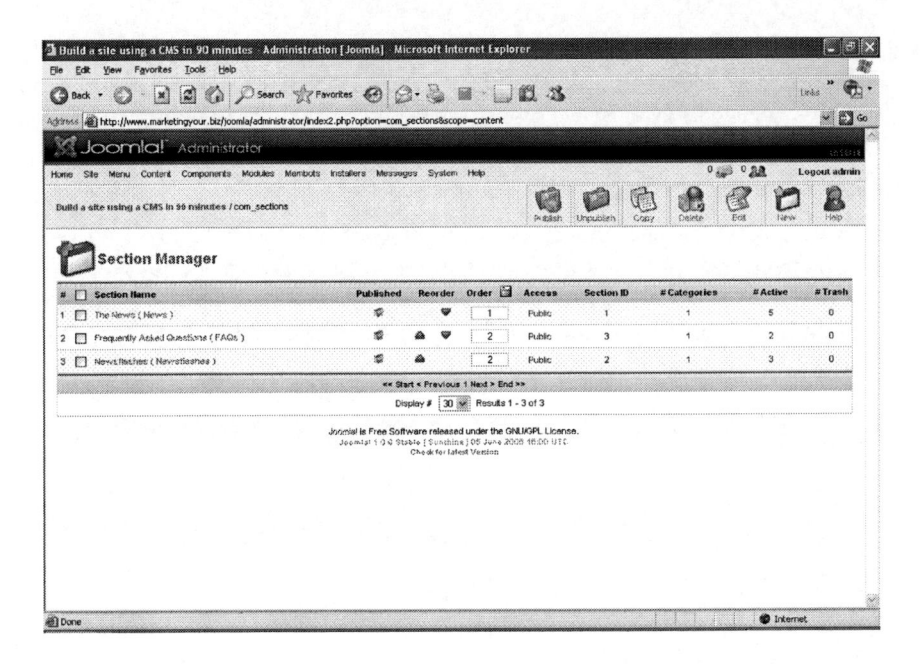

5.2. The section manager gives immediate information about the created section and number of categories underneath them

The page above contains three sections. The 'published' icon allows sections to be enabled or disabled at the click of a mouse. Sections can be reordered either by clicking on the blue sort icons or by entering the sequence you require and clicking on the small floppy disc icon next to Order. The four columns to the right provide the ID of the section, then number of categories within each section, number of active items within the section and the number of trashed items.

To create a new section click on New. The next screen then prompts you to enter various pieces of information. Whether you need this information depends on whether you intend to link directly to this section, or instead to categories or content items. You don't need to worry about this too much at this stage – we'll cover this in detail later on, and you can always come back and modify this information later. For now, enter a title and section name (these can be the same). Next, select an image from the dropdown menu – you are limited to images in the root Images directory, and you can design your own image set if desired. Select the access level for this category (e.g. whether users must be registered or require 'special' access to gain entry to all content within this section). Next, enter a description of the section.

To the right you will notice an area entitled MOSimage Directories. This allows you to allocate a directory that that be used by items within this section – this is useful when you have a large collection of images which will be separated by section and category.

Click on Apply (*not* Save at this stage).

To the right there will now be a quick method to add a link to your new section from a menu – you can also use the Menu option from the dropdown menu, but let's add it into the menu for now. Select 'mainmenu', then section list from the dropdown menu. Lastly, enter a name for your menu and click on the 'link to menu' button.

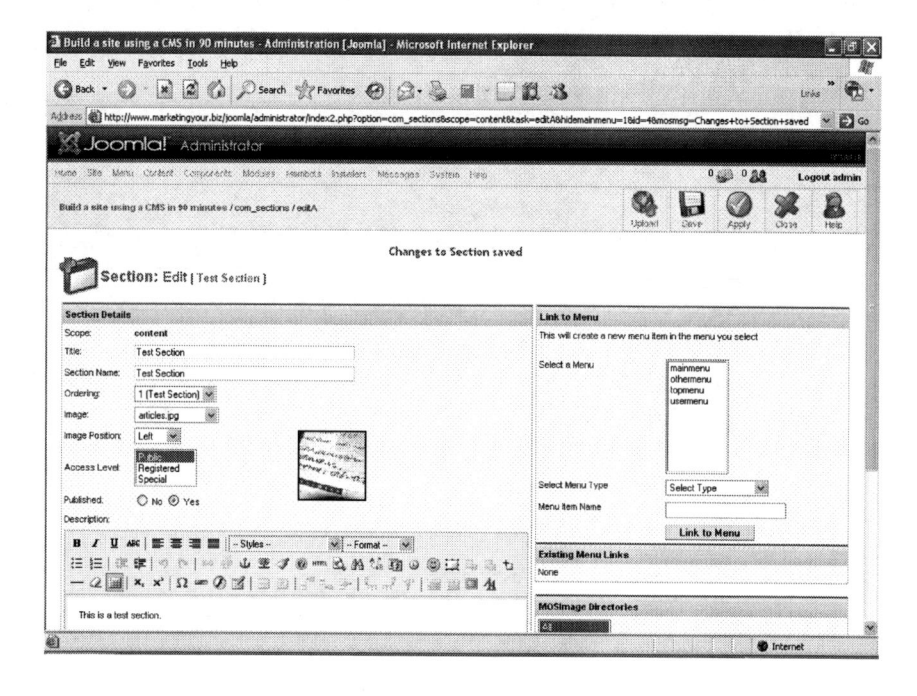

5.3. Creating a section in Joomla!

If you preview your site, you will see that you have a new menu item with your section name listed. Clicking on the link will display the section, with the title, image and text you just typed. If there were subcategories that had content in they would be listed underneath. The format of these listings would be determined on the menu type you selected on the previous screen.

Structuring Your Content

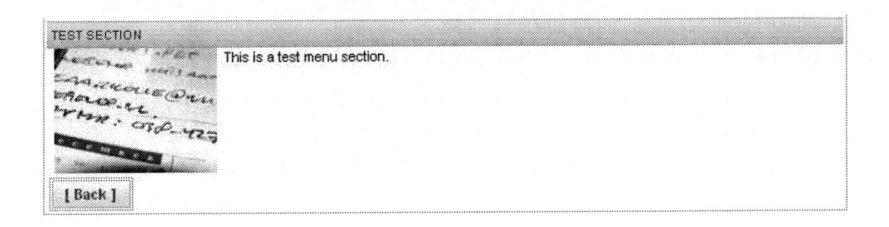

5.4. Your completed section, as viewed when clicked on the created menu link

Creating your categories

So, we have our section in place, now we need to create our categories. This process is virtually identical to creating a section. Go to the Category Manager either from the icon on the home page or through the menu, and then click on New. The next screen displayed will be rather familiar, however now you can select your section from the dropdown menu.

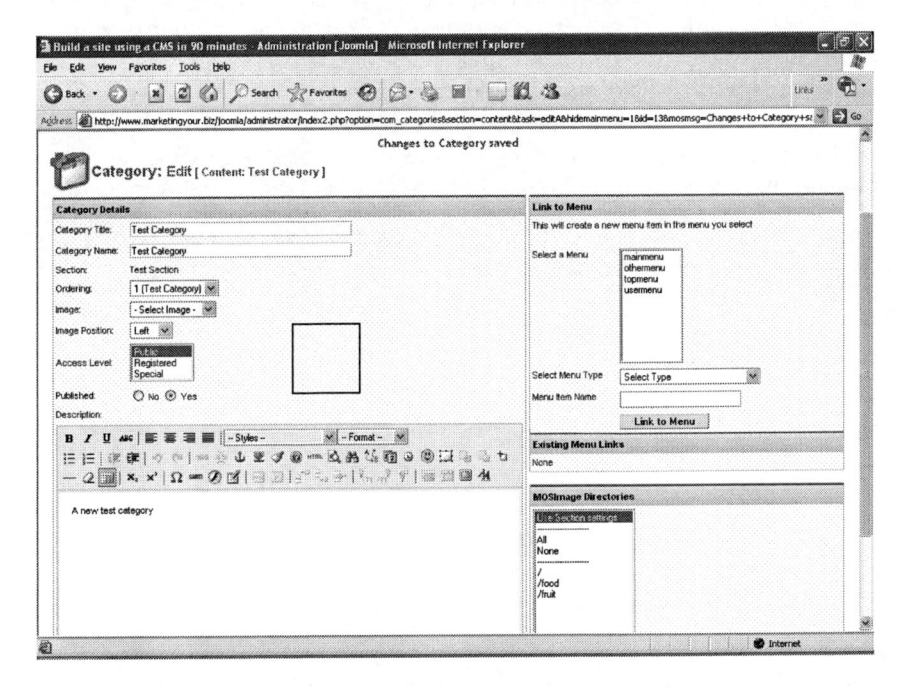

5.5 Creating a category is much the same as creating a section

As before, the MOSImage Directories allow you to further limit the graphics that will be available when creating content within any given category.

In the process of creating the category (but only after saving or applying) you will see that you again have the option to add a link to the menu. This clearly demonstrates the point made earlier that you can place menu links to your content from any level – section, category or content item.

If you were to preview your site and again click on the section link it would look no different to what it looked like before the creation of the new subcategory. Why? Joomla! is intelligent enough to know that there are no items within the subcategory, so there is no point in showing the category at all.

You can create pages outside of this structure – this is known as Static Content, and is covered in more detail in the next chapter.

Summary

Joomla! provides a comprehensive method of categorising your site, but it can be quite daunting at first. Remember that what you create now is not caste in stone – you could simply create one section with one category, then break it down as the site grows, relocating content into new sections at the click of a mouse. It is essential that you understand that the categorising of content through sections and categories is a separate issue to that of creating menus, although of course the two are inextricably linked.

6. Adding Content

Now we get to the good stuff! Adding content is what Joomla! is all about. As we are adding a new item we could simply click on the 'Add new content' icon on the front page – this will take you directly to a blank content page. Alternatively, click on Content, then Content by Section followed by any of the sections displayed. Each sub menu has two options – a list of items or the ability to add or edit the categories within this section. You would want the top option. This would display a screen which details all items, along with their categories.

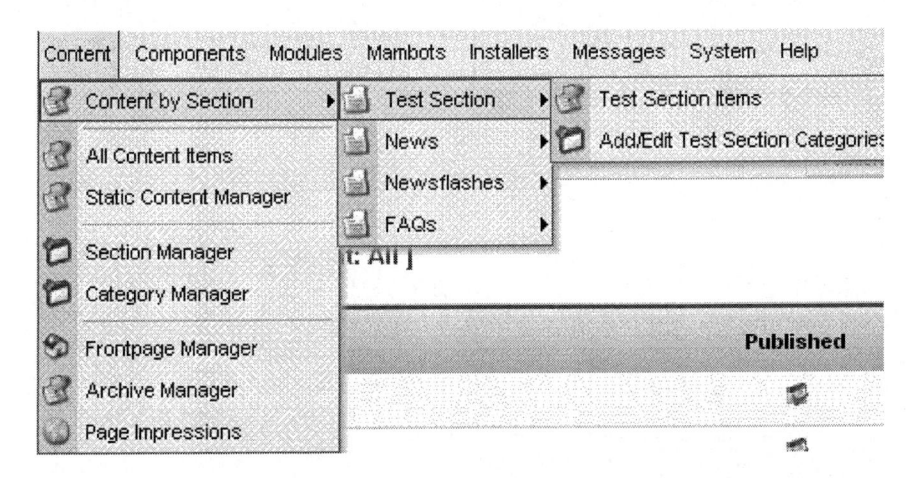

6.1 As new sections are created you can add or amend content within them through the drop-down menus

If you took the drop-down menu route then you need to click on New. The benefit of taking the longer route is that Joomla! knows that you want to create a new item in a specific section, and so populates the section dropdown field accordingly.

Building a Website Using a CMS in 90 Minutes

6.2. The most important screen within Joomla! – Creating new content

The New Content Item screen consists of two main blocks – item details on the left and the parameters (tabbed) block on the right. The title, section, category, intro text and main content appear in the left area. The tabbed section allows you to tweak various parameters – these will be covered in detail later.

Item details

Title: The name which is displayed above a content item and in table or blog views (which shows the intro text and a link to the full item – see fig 6.5) of a category. Ensure that any title you use is descriptive and, where possible, contains keywords that you expect users would use to locate pages containing content such as yours. This is covered in more detail in chapter 11 on search engine optimisation.

Adding Content

Title alias: This field is not currently in use by the main Joomla! core, but some search engine friendly (SEF) applications use this for meta tags. Simply duplicate the text you place in the title.

Section: A drop-down menu showing all sections – if you entered via the dropdown menu then the section will already be entered.

Category: Allows selection of a category within a section. As you change the sections dropdown the categories dropdown will only display the categories within the selected section.

Intro text: Type here the introductory portion of the content. This is the part displayed in Blog Lists for both Categories and Sections. In other words this text can be displayed on other pages as a lead into this content item. It can also be configured to be hidden when you view the content.

Main text: This is the body of your content. It is only shown when viewing that content in full view, and is not shown in Blog Lists.

You will no doubt have noted the two identical toolbars above the intro and main sections. These work in the same way as your word processor and provide new users with an interface to format text in almost an identical way to what they are already used to.

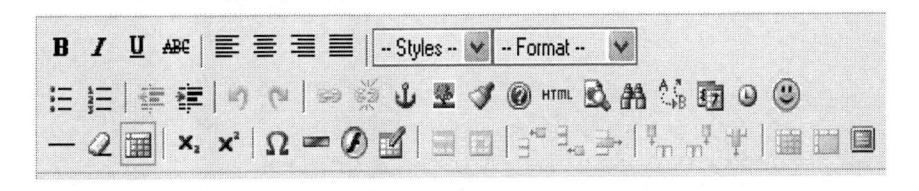

6.3. The toolbar gives users plenty of tools to apply styles to content.

In addition to the usual bold, italics, alignment and bullets/indents, you can also add hyperlinks, images, search content, edit html and much more.

Note: The editor supplied as standard (TinyMCE) is not the most feature-packed editor available. Try installing TMEDIT instead – this is even better, and provides an extremely easy method of inserting and editing graphics. Googling TMEDIT Joomla should throw up enough sources for you to locate it.

The tabbed menu

Rather than give you an in-depth description of each field within each of the tabbed menus, let's instead concentrate on what you need to know immediately, and then revisit relevant options as they are needed later on. Let's start by describing what each menu covers in general:

Publishing: Allows you to decide when an item will start and finish being available, who can access it and whether it is also displayed on the front page.

Images: One method of inserting images. As mentioned above, if you install TMEDIT one of the better features it provides is a much easier method of image insertion. The standard method using this tab is described further on, however.

Parameters: Allows configuration of how the article is displayed, including page title, whether section/category names are displayed/linked, display of print, pdf and email icons etc.

Meta Info: Allows keyword and description meta tags to be added to each page, providing extra information to search engines.

Link to menu: Provides a quick method of adding a link from a menu to the page you are creating.

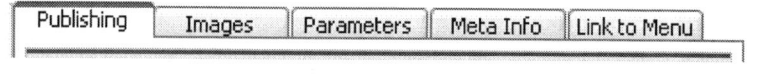

6.4. The tabbed toolbar

The process of constructing a page of content

If the last few pages have made your eyes glaze over a little, then let's take a more practical approach to what you might do to create a page of content, perhaps including a few graphics, make the page more search engine friendly and changing some of the standard parameters.

Step 1: Title and Category

Click on Add New Content from the home page and enter a title for your page. Keep the title down to 3-6 words, and try to use words that will immediately identify the content on the page – search engines rank keywords in the title highly. Now select the section and subsequent category – only categories within the section you select will be displayed. You can either leave the Title Alias field blank or copy and paste the title here – at present this field is not used by Joomla!

Adding Content

Step 2: Introductory text
If you intend to either display content in the 'Blog' format or publish snippets of stories on the front page of your site then you need to think carefully about your introduction text. Limit it to two or three lines of text which act as a good enticement into the main story.

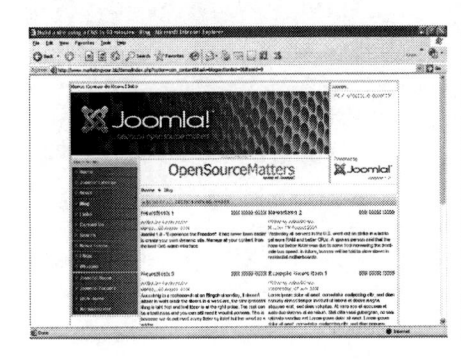

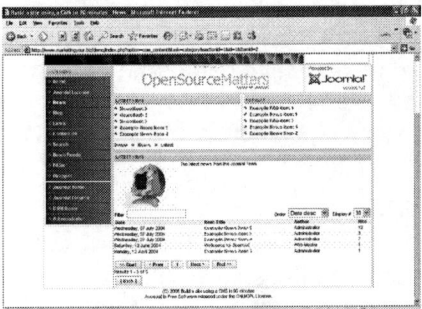

6.5. The introductory text is displayed when viewed in 'Blog view' (left) but only the title is displayed in table view (right)

Step 3: Main text
This area holds the main content and works in exactly the same way as the intro field above. When a user clicks on the 'More...' button from an intro item, or from a link elsewhere to this item, then both the Intro and main content sections are displayed.

Word-pasting Woes
You will either be writing your content from scratch or cutting/pasting from a word processor or other source. If the latter you may have to do some reformatting. MS Word has a bad habit of inserting formatting code which is not always immediately noticeable (unless you can read HTML and go into the source code, which is not recommended for the uninitiated). One great trick is to copy text from MS Word into Windows Notepad – this strips out all text formatting. Now copy and paste it from Notepad into your Joomla! intro or main content window and you can use the toolbar to format it as desired. This can be a minor annoyance if your document is formatted correctly in Word but does not transmit correctly when you paste it into Joomla!

Step 4: Publishing settings
You will know if you intend to publish the intro text of this item on the front page, so check this box if required. All items are published by default (meaning that they will go live as soon as you save them) – if you are working on a page which is not yet finished then untick this box. You can

then go back to work on it at your leisure without it being accessible from the frontend of the site. Select the access level for the content. If you want to change the name of the author displayed (which is taken from your registered name), change it in the next field. You can also assign ownership of the article to someone else, which is useful for those who you have perhaps not given administration rights to, but who need to edit some content.

While you can change the ordering of items, this is not really necessary at this stage, as the category content list has up/down arrows for easily relocating content. You can also change the ordering of items when editing menu items.

Next you can set/change the start and finish dates, along with overriding the date of publication from now (default) to a date forward or back in time, useful perhaps if you are migrating content from an old site and don't want to list a current creation date.

Step 5: Adding Images

Before inserting images you to need upload them. If you are transferring an existing site to Joomla! then the easiest method is to transfer the files using FTP software to the default '\images\stories\' folder (created during installation), which will then make them accessible from the content creation page. Where you have a larger number of images you may want to create relevant subfolders and upload images to each of them. If you want to upload images as you add your content this

6.6. An image selected and made 'active' using the standard method of inserting graphics

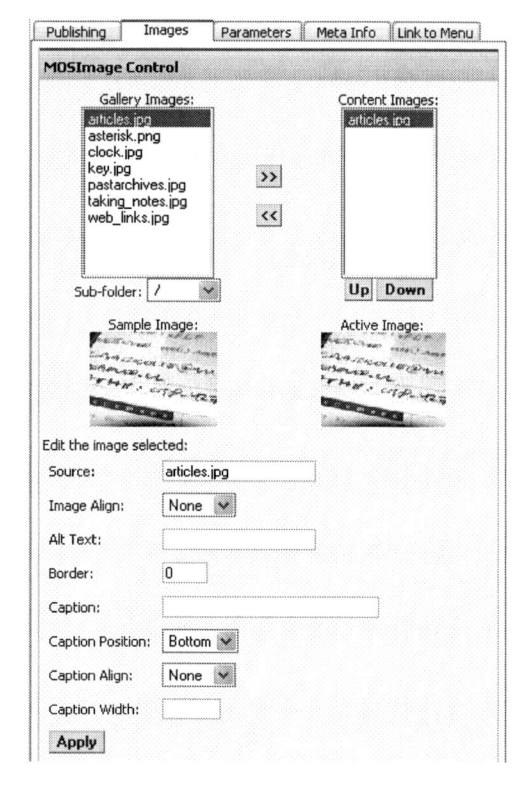

Adding Content

is also quite straightforward. In the top right menu bar click on the Upload button, and use the Browse button in the pop-up window to locate the file on your hard disc, then click Upload to transfer the file. It will then appear in your Gallery list in the root stories folder.

Inserting your images is a slightly more convoluted process. There are actually two methods of adding images within a standard Joomla! installation – through the tab menu on the right or using the Insert Image icon within the toolbar above the intro and main sections.

Let's start by explaining the tabbed menu method, for which we'll use the images installed with the sample data. When selecting the Images tab on the right, you will see two boxes – Gallery images and Content images. Select the image you want to insert from the Gallery list, which displays a thumbnail image underneath the list, and then click on the right arrow – it then appears in the Content images box. Click on it and you'll see another thumbnail. Now change any of the parameters below – this will normally at least consist of adding ALT text, specifying a border and setting/changing the image alignment – the last is important. Click on Apply to save these settings. Now position your cursor at the start of the line where you want your image to appear – remember that if you set your alignment to Right you can still set the cursor to the left as it will wrap the text to the left of it automatically. Finally, click on Insert Image – a small icon just below the text content area – this will insert the text {mosimage} within the text. Joomla! knows that this marker is where you want your image and will insert it accordingly. You can repeat this process for as many images as you want in either your intro or main text – just add them to the Content image box, change the settings for each, click on Apply and then click Insert Image with the cursor in the right place. Image order can be changed by clicking on Up/Down under Content Images. Joomla! will insert each image in turn each time it comes across {mosimage} within a content item.

The second method is to use the WYSIWYG 'insert image' icon, provided by the TinyMCE editor, shipped as standard with Joomla! Clicking on this displays a dialog box which prompts you to enter a complete URL for the image, which is not really that user-friendly! The tabbed view provides a wider variety of options, including adding in code automatically to swap images when the mouse is rolled over. Once you have entered the relevant information click on Insert, which will place the image into your document.

Unlike the previous method you will actually see the image within your document and can even resize it. If you need to change any setting just click on the image and then the Insert Image icon, which will bring up the same dialog box but with the field populated with the image's information. This method of image insertion is only likely to be preferred by advanced users.

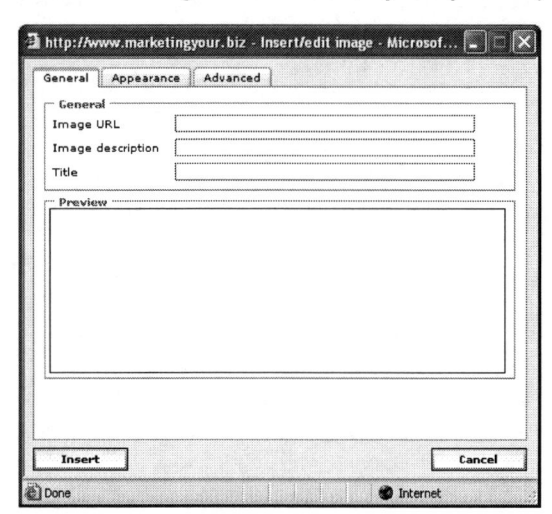

6.7. The standard toolbar image insertion icon is not the easiest method to add images

Adding images the easy way!
If you have installed TMEDIT then adding images is a much less taxing process. Within the intro or main toolbars you will see an image icon (bottom row – third image in from left). Click on this to bring up a pop-up window that will then display all the files and folders within the \images\stories folder. You navigate this as you would with Windows Explorer, with thumbnails of your sub-folders and images being displayed. Clicking on an image will populate the path and dimension fields underneath. You can then add in any other information, such as ALT text, image size, horizontal/vertical spacing, border etc. You can also use this screen to upload images. As you can see this is altogether a much more logical and simple way of managing images – one screen does it all, and much more graphically than the previous two.

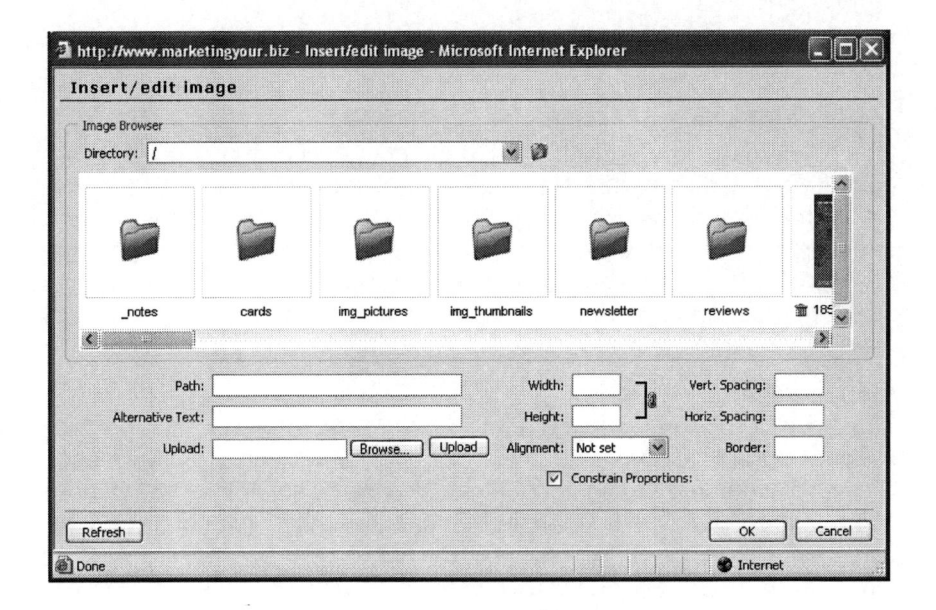

*6.8. Adding images with TMEDIT is much easier
than the standard image insertion process*

Step 6: Modifying Parameters to change the look and feel of the page
For the CSS gurus amongst you it is possible to add in a suffix to add in more CSS to change the look of elements on this page, although it is unlikely that many will need to do this. Most of the next options are either show/hide options or show/hide/use global settings. Chances are that the default settings (specified in the global configuration section) will be fine for you for most pages. Other parameters covered include the display of the back button, pdf, print and email icons, item ratings, author name, date published/modified.

Step 7: Add your META tags
This is very important for your search engine optimisation. Add in a description and keywords relevant to the specific page. They may include general words that are relevant to your entire site, but should mainly focus on the page itself. Clicking on the Add Sect/Cat/Title will append the section name, category name and title to the keywords section.

Note: There are add-on 'mambots' available that will automatically scan pages and add words that appear frequently into your Meta tags. If you want to automate the process then consider installing one. A good mambot to

Building a Website Using a CMS in 90 Minutes

consider is 'botMetaFly', which is available in the extensions sections of the Joomla! web site.

Step 8: Add a link to a menu

This option gives you a quick method of adding a link to the newly created page from any menu, rather than going the long route round of clicking on the menu dropdown, selecting the menu and following the screens afterwards. You might want to use this facility if, for example, the page you are creating is a main page of interest, such as an 'About Us' page. Just select the menu you wish to add the item to, and then enter the text you want to appear in the menu. Click on Link to menu, and you are done.

Step 9: Save!

It may sound obvious, but you do also have to save your work after this – clicking on the tabs on the right does not apply any of the changes until you click on Save in the top-right menu bar. You can also click on Apply at any point – this saves your changes without returning you to the content category listings, which is useful if you want to save and continue editing. Once saved, if you designated an item as 'published' then it will immediately appear on your site and be accessible through the 'search site' facility.

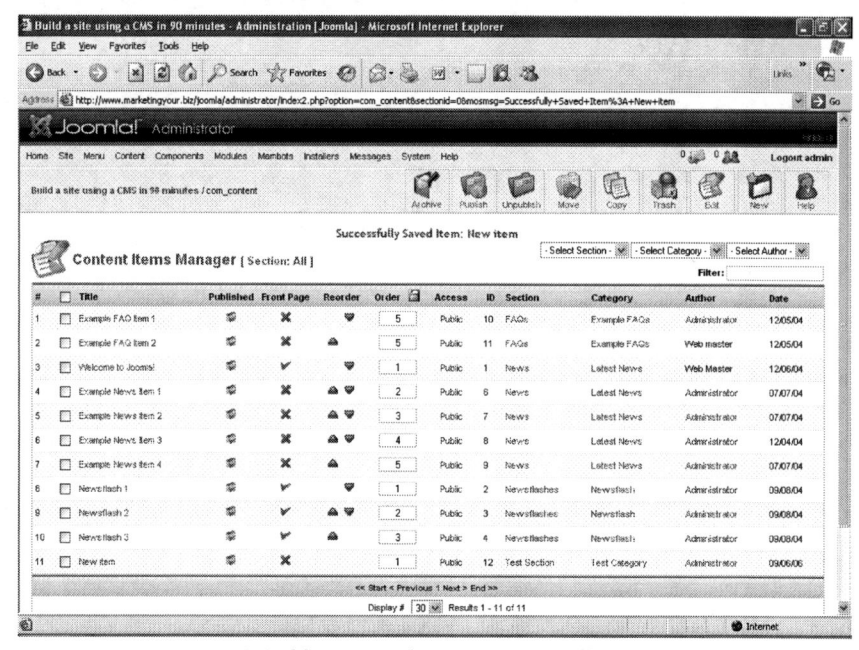

6.9. Your new items are now listed

Adding Content

Static content
There may be occasions where you do not wish to create pages within sections and categories. Maybe instead of having a category for company pages you might create static pages (e.g. About Us, Terms and Conditions etc). For this reasons Joomla allows the creation of 'static pages'. The process of creating static content is exactly the same as described for categorised content, with two exceptions – you can only link to static content items from a menu and cannot display it on the front page. Static pages will be included within search results if users employ the site's search facility.

Lastly, it is worth noting that although the editor within the content creation page allows you to dip into the HTML, you cannot add complex code (such as JavaScript). If you are trying to convert some pages that have complex code that will not migrate, you can overcome this by linking to the page from a menu using the 'wrapper' function. Simply create a page with your code on, save it somewhere on your site and then create a menu item linking to a wrapper page – now enter the URL of the page you just uploaded. There may be an alternative in the form of a mambot – always search the Joomla! extensions section or the forums to see if anyone else has encountered the same issue and found a solution. One such example is adding in the code for Google Adsense banners and text-based adverts – you cannot cut/paste Google's code, but fortunately there is a mambot that handles this.

Archiving Content
You may have noticed a button on the content list marked 'Archive' (fig 6.9) – you can move old items here once they are no longer needed in their existing sections or categories. You can then create a link to an archived section or category content. This ensures that important content is not cluttered by out-of-date content, but the older material is still available.

Summary
Creating content within Joomla! is very simple, using an interface that is instantly familiar to anyone that uses a web browser and a word processor. Once you have your site configured, the process of adding content requires users with only basic computer skills. If you are trying to add complex HTML this can initially be a problem, but given the size of the Mambo/Joomla! community, there is generally someone who has encountered the same issue and worked a way around it. Using the wrapper facility allows you to pull in content from external pages.

7. Security and Access Restrictions

During the content creating process, we discussed allocating an access level – it is this hierarchy that we are discussing now, and how you can use it to allow or restrict access to users and site administrators.

If everyone visiting your website is to have access to everything without registration, and you are the only person that requires access to the back end administration section, then you will not use groups, however it is worthwhile spending the time to understand them.

To understand the concept of security access, there is no better place to start than the user manager section. Click on the User Manager link from the front page, followed by New.

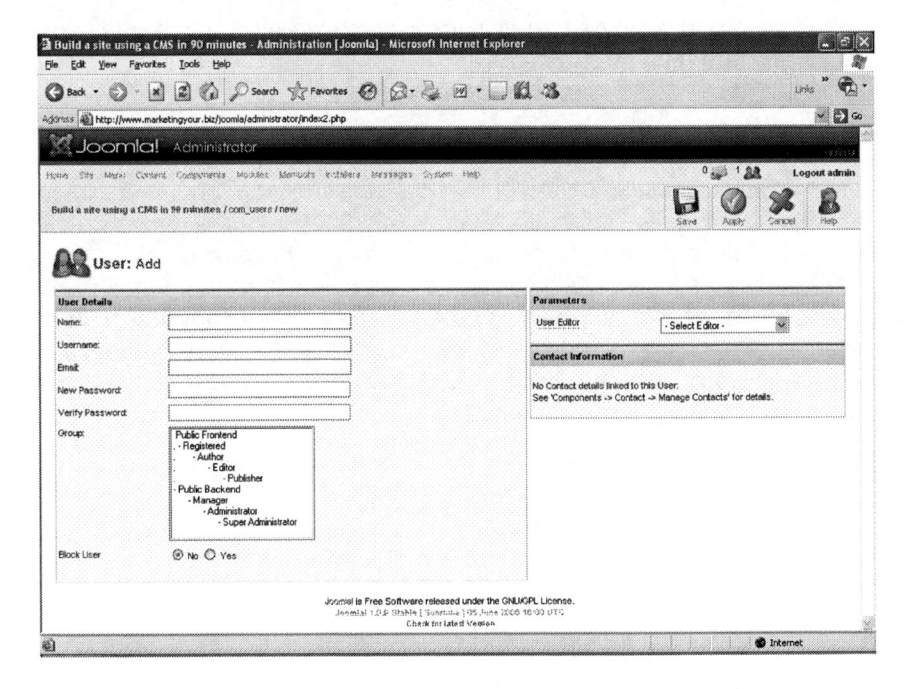

7.1 The user creation screen, showing the various groups

What you need to focus on is the 'Group' box – you will see two main sections: Public Frontend and Public Backend, each with their own sub-options. Let's start with the Frontend. Note that casual visitors do not fall into any of these categories – it is only for those that register or that are created by you. There are four options within this group, which only apply to visitors that log into the front of your web site.

Registered:
Users that have a status of 'registered' have access to any material that has this status appended to it. This is the next level up from a basic visitor to the site. Most sites will only require this level of separation between users.

Author:
Authors can see/do everything that a registered user can as well as submit new information, usually via a link in the user menu. New content will require authorisation from a manager or administrator.

Editor:
Can see/do everything that an author can. Can also post and edit any content item from the front end.

Publisher:
A publisher can post, edit and publish any content item from the front end.

All of the above access levels only allow users to control content pages within the frontend. So, for example, they could not see other users' details, install/uninstall components, modules or mambots, or remove menu items. From a security perspective, while some access levels have the potential to allow users to modify their own or others' content, they cannot modify the fundamental elements of the site. Adding trusted users to a higher level is a great way to spread the burden of adding and maintaining content, thus allowing the site to grow exponentially.

Public backend access:
The backend administration section allows a much greater level of control over your site. There are only three levels of access levels for the backend:

Manager:
Have access to some backend and all frontend actions. A manager won't for example be able to install new components.

Administrator:
Cannot delete super administrators but can perform all frontend and most backend functions.

Super Administrator:
Has access to all frontend and backend functions.

Security and Access Restrictions

The Special User Parameter:
When you create content or menu items, you only have three access levels available – Public, Registered or Special – despite there being seven access levels in total. Any user created as Author, Editor, Publisher, Manager, Administrator or Super Administrator is considered a Special User. They can submit news, articles, FAQs and Web Links. These Special Users are the only ones able to access to an item with the 'Special' access parameter from the frontend. Special users are the only ones to see on screen menu items or entire menus with the 'Special' access parameter.

It is especially useful if you publish the 'User Menu' Module, which is often used to give a single group of menu options for special users. The entire module may be hidden from any 'Public' or 'Registered' user by specifying its access as 'Special'.

User Registration Activation:
When a visitor wants to register an account with your site, this is done through the 'register button' within the Login Form. They are then prompted for Name, Username, E-mail and Password.

When they submit the registration request, the account is created but by default the user cannot login until the account is activated. An e-mail with the activation link is sent to the email address provided by the visitor. When the mail is received, the user will click the activation link, the account will be activated and the user will now be able to log in.

This feature has several advantages:
- It verifies that visitor exists and has a valid E-mail address.
- It gives the user the ability to choose their password at registration.
- It gives the site administrators a better overview of activated and non-activated accounts. A non-activated account will appear as blocked and never signed in. As such it is easy to track and delete.

7.2. User registration is a simple process

57

The option for Registration Activation is found in Global Configuration under the Site tab. See the option for 'Use New Account Activation'. If you disable user activation, visitors will be able to log in immediately after they created an account.

A simple test

Understanding these user levels can be difficult for the uninitiated, so try this simple task to better understand how user level affect your web site:

1. Create a page of content and leave it set as public access
2. Make sure you can access this page on your website
3. Now go back to the backend, open the previously created page and change it to Registered access
4. Return to the frontend and the page will disappear when you refresh it
5. Register a new account (from the frontend) and activate it using the email that you will receive
6. Log in and the page will reappear

Repeat the above process, but instead of registering an account in the frontend, go to the administration section and create users with author, editor and publisher attributes. Now take a look at the additional icons that appear on different pages and sections of the site and the level of control it provides each user.

Summary

If you plan for your site to grow rapidly, then providing users with access to edit or add content reduces your own workload whilst maintaining security over more sensitive control of the site. Before allocating users with special access levels ensure that you understand exactly what they will be gaining access to. If you are the only administrator and you want all pages to be accessible to all users, or only public user/registered user separation is required then you need not spend too much time understanding the other access levels.

8. The Media Manager

We discussed adding images to content in chapter 6, but there will also be a need for greater image management as your site grows. Maybe you want to create sub-folders for specific sections or categories and upload graphics to here, so that your main directory does not get too cluttered. Or perhaps you need to delete old or unused images. The Media Manager is the place to perform these functions, and is accessible either from the initial logged-in screen or from the Site dropdown menu.

Note: You can only upload certain files with the Media Manager, namely .bmp, .gif, .jpg, .png, .doc, .xls, .pdf and .swf – in other words just pictures, Macromedia Flash files, documents or spreadsheets. All other file types would need to be uploaded through FTP software. The best example of another file type you might want to upload would be an MP3 audio file.

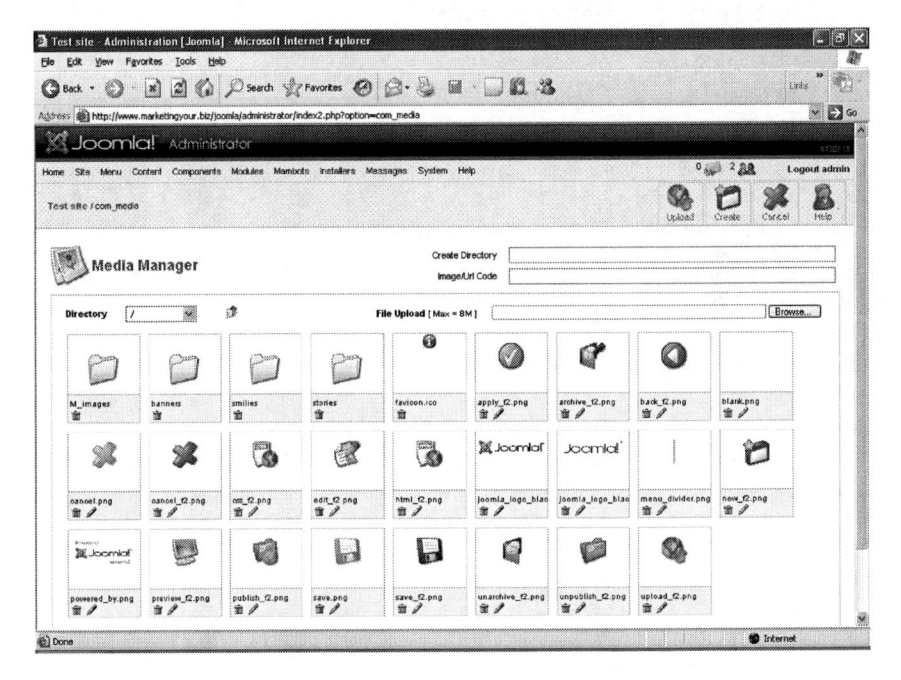

8.1. The Media Manager main screen

Using the Media Manager is simple enough. You are presented with a view of the \images folder, with all sub-folders and thumbnail images of images. Each image and folder has a delete button underneath it (although you cannot delete a folder unless it is emptied first). Images also have a small pencil icon, which will copy the full URL to the image/URL code field above, allowing easy insertion using the standard TinyMCE image insert facility – this also occurs when you click on an image. Clicking on a folder will open it and show any images and sub-folders within it.

It is worthwhile getting into the habit of creating subfolders and storing specific graphics within them. As your site grows, a single folder with hundreds of graphics soon becomes unwieldy. The Media Manager also lacks the ability to move files from one location to another.

Creating a new folder
Simply enter the name of the folder into the field marked 'Create Directory' and click on the Create icon in the top right menu bar. The screen will refresh and your new folder is available.

Uploading a file
Go to the folder in which you want to place your image, and then click on the Browse button on the right. Select your file and click on Open – this places the path to the file in the field. Now click on the Upload button in the button bar top right of the screen – the file will now upload, the screen will refresh and a thumbnail image of your file will be displayed.

Note: Don't forget that when inserting graphics within content, the pop-up windows only search from the default \images\stories folder and those below it. Therefore if you upload a graphic before going into the \stories subfolder it won't be visible when you try to add it to a content item.

When to use FTP over the Media Manager
For 95% of jobs, the Media Manager offers a quick and robust solution, however there are some occasions when FTP is generally the better option. Firstly, if you need to upload large files, the Media Manager limits you to 8MB. Next you are restricted to the file types mentioned earlier.

A more powerful alternative
For those who are comfortable with FTP software, but perhaps do not have access, or would prefer to do everything within Joomla!, there is a component available that you should consider installing – Joomla! Explorer. This free component effectively turns your web browser into an FTP client, giving you complete access to all of your files and folders. You can cut,

copy, paste, rename or delete files *en masse*. Use with caution though – a couple of careless clicks could delete an entire folder, and there's no undo feature!

Summary

The Media Manager gives users a familiar interface in which to upload images and documents to the site. Use subfolder structures wisely to ensure that your main \stories folder does not become too clogged with images. Advanced users may also want to consider installing the Joomla! Explorer component for added functionality.

9. Installing Templates

With the loading of each page, Joomla! is performing a myriad calculations based on the components installed and the preferences set. The most visible function is when it drops this information into the places you specify within a pre-defined template.

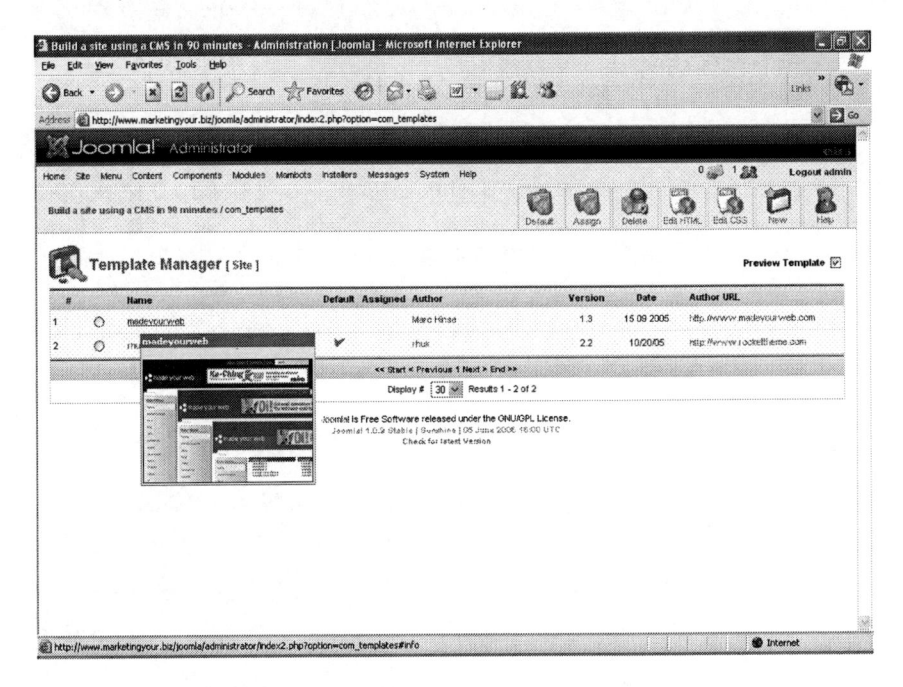

9.1 The Site Template Manager, showing a thumbnail image of the template selected as Default

There are literally thousands of different template designs, as Mambo and Joomla! templates are (currently) interchangeable. Many are free, but some are chargeable, with the minor benefit being that the latter are likely to be a little more exclusive. Normally you will only be looking at a nominal fee of £10-20, so if you want to ensure that your site does not potentially look the same as 1000 others out there, it may be worth the investment (given that up until now you've probably only paid for your web space!)

There are two types of templates for Joomla! – site templates and administrator templates, however it is recommended that you only use the former. Site templates only affect the frontend – in other words only what your general users will see. Administrator templates affect the back end. Bear in mind that as soon as you change your administrator template, any documentation or tutorials that you see relating to Joomla! (such as the online help, and even this book) will no longer resemble the screens that anyone using the backend administration screens will see. This will make it more difficult to train new users using existing material, and there is no real reason to do it other than for aesthetic reasons. Therefore this book only covers frontend templates.

Finding new templates

A quick 'Google' of 'free Joomla templates' will throw up thousands of sites. Your job now is simply to trawl through them, looking at whatever thumbnail images they show for a template and, if you like it, follow the links to download them. Some sites may require registration, and you should already be familiar with this process as they will no doubt be Joomla!-powered sites.

When downloading templates, they will always be supplied as a zip file – you need do nothing to it. Don't even unpack it. During the uploading process Joomla will read an XML format file included within the zip which contains an index of all the files within the template and where they should be placed.

Below are just a few sites that you may want to visit in your search for the perfect template:

- → www.joomlashack.com
- → www.joomla-templates.com
- → www.mambohut.com
- → www.joomlart.com
- → www.joomlahacks.com
- → www.joomladesigns.co.uk
- → www.joomplates.com

One site worthy of a special mention is joomladesigns.co.uk, which charges a flat annual fee (currently of ⌂25) to access their database of 100+ templates. What also separates this site is that it also supplies the source PhotoShop graphics for further customisation.

Installing your new template file

As with components, mambots and modules, the installation of a template is a simple process. Click on the Installers menu bar option then select site templates. You'll be presented with a screen inviting you to browse for your

Installing Templates

downloaded zip file. Locate it and select Install. You should be greeted with a 'Success' screen. Click on the Continue button to return to the list of installed templates.

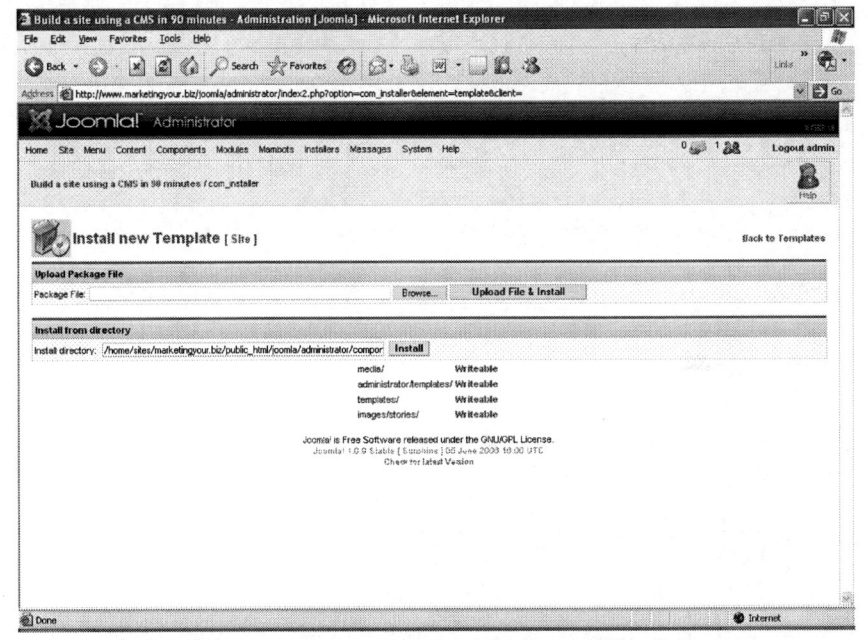

9.2. Installing a template takes just a few clicks of the mouse

If your server does not support GZIP with PHP then you can simply unzip the file and upload it to \Templates\ – ensure that you insert the files in a subfolder of \Templates, usually named after the template you are installing – e.g. \Templates\My_Template.

Note: Sometimes a zip file might contain several different versions or colours of a template. If you get a 'failure' notice when you try to install a template, open the zip file and see whether it has several other zip files inside it. If it has, chances are that you'll have to unzip the main file and try to install one of the other zips to get the template/colour you want.

Next you have to 'assign' your template to pages within your site. It is normal to simply make it the default template for all pages to use, but you can actually create different templates and apply them to different pages. If yours is a new site with no pages added, then you can just click on the Default button. Refer back to figure 9.1 to see the Default/Assigned columns and icons.

Building a Website Using a CMS in 90 Minutes

To test your new template you can either manually open a new browser and enter your URL or click on Site, Preview, Preview in new Window.

Modifying an existing template

Most users will find a template that meets 90% of their needs but requires customising to fit in with existing requirements – perhaps the graphics do not match, or you need to add or modify module positions. Joomla! provides backend access to both the main HTML layout code and the CSS code for templates, meaning that you can easily change the look of a site. Click on Site, Preview and Inline with positions and you will be presented with an outline of your site with the various module positions highlighted. This shows you where certain elements will be placed when the page is loaded.

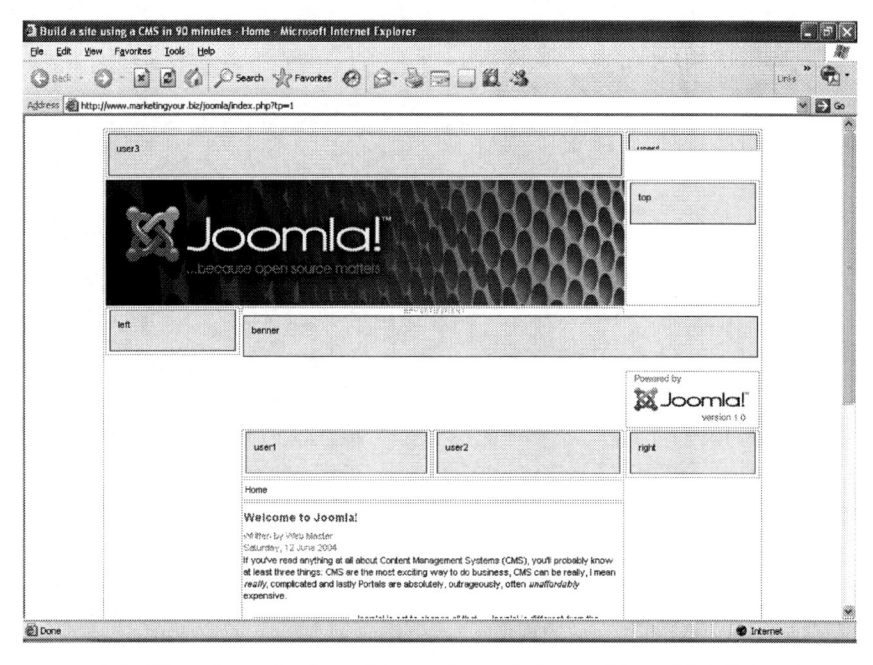

9.3. The view of a template with module positions highlighted

To modify either the HTML or CSS of a site does require reasonable skills in both languages. To edit these elements click on Site, Template Manager and Site Templates. Tick the radio box to the left of your template and select Edit HTML from the top-right toolbar. You will now be presented with the source code in an editable window. EDIT THIS WITH CARE, AND KEEP A BACKUP LOCALLY AS ALL SAVED CHANGES WILL IMMEDIATELY BE MADE LIVE ON YOUR SITE.

Installing Templates

The same process also applies to editing the CSS content. Again, select your template and now click on Edit CSS to be greeted with the CSS content. You may of course prefer to download both files and edit them in your chosen HTML editor, but be mindful to keep a separate backup of both files in case of emergency.

You may also need to edit the images associated with the template – these are generally stored in a subfolder called \images from within your \Templates\Your Template Name\. Download these, edit accordingly and re-upload. If the images' dimensions change then you may need to make additional changes to your CSS and HTML files.

You can add in your own module positions to a template. Let's say that the template you've chosen does not have an area for a legal disclaimer and you want to add one. Under Site\Template Manager there is an option entitled Module Positions. This lists 27 pre-defined positions that developers adhere to, one of which is called 'legals'. Now open the source code of your template, locate the area you want to insert your module position and add in:

<?php mosLoadModules ('legals'); ?>

At this stage you will not notice any difference to your site, however if you now go into Modules\Site Modules and click on the module name that you want to reposition, you can select 'legals' from the module position dropdown menu. Once saved, refresh your site and you'll see that your module is now in its new location.

Allowing users to choose their own template

One of the modules in Joomla! is called the Template Chooser. From the dropdown menu you can choose one of the installed templates. Selecting a new one causes a new thumbnail images to load, so before you click on the OK button you can get an idea of whether it is even worth you loading the full page. To enable this module go to Modules, Site Modules and ensure that Template Chooser is published to a viewable location (e.g. Left, Right etc). You can change where it is displayed by selecting the module from the list and changing the position from the dropdown menu. Many sites that sell templates use this to allow visitors to try out a template.

10. Making Your Own Joomla! Template

Before we even start to discuss this topic it should be noted that only readers that are skilled with HTML and CSS should attempt to write their own template. If you want to create a custom design you are far better off trying to find a free or low-cost template that meets most of your needs, and then changing some of the graphics to suit. This will be a much quicker, painless and less error-prone process.

There are three areas you need to consider when designing your template – usability, search engine optimisation and accessibility. Usability is handled by the navigation that you specify within Joomla!, along with your placement of modules. Search engine optimisation and accessibility often go hand in hand with generating clean code – if your site is W3C compliant, then the code should be lean, which in turn will be better for both search engines and visitors with special accessibility needs.

If you are dead set on creating your own template, or need to convert a HTML site to Joomla! then there is a great tool that can make the job easier. You will, however require Macromedia Dreamweaver MX or higher in order to use it. Do a Google search for mambosolutions453.mxp – this is a Dreamweaver 'extension' that adds a toolbar which allows you to drop in the relevant code into a standard HTML page to insert the various pieces of code required. You will also need the Macromedia Extension Manager. This should be installed automatically with Dreamweaver – if not check your installation CD or the Macromedia web site.

Once you've downloaded the extension, double click on the file to install it. Now open Dreamweaver. Usually the 'common' tab is displayed at the top. Click on it and select Mambosolutions453 from the list. You should now see the following toolbar:

10.1. The Mambosolutions453 toolbar

The structure of a Joomla! template
As you discovered in the previous chapter, Joomla! templates are generally supplied as a single zip file. These file contain the following:

- **index.php** – this is the page that contains the physical HTML that structures your page layout
- **template_thumbnail.png** – small graphical image of your template that is displayed either in the backend admin section or, if enabled, in the template chooser module
- **templateDetails.xml** – a file that contains information about which files are used for the template and their location, along with author information
- **templates_css.css** – stored in a subfolder called css, this file contains all of the cascading style sheet information about your site
- **additional graphics** – all template graphics are stored in an images subfolder

Note: This book assumes that you do not have a test server set up locally. You will therefore need to create all of the elements of your template and install it in the usual fashion before testing can begin. It is best to install beta templates on a test site rather than a live site.

Starting your page

Start by creating a blank page within Dreamweaver. Go to the code view and delete any basic HTML code that Dreamweaver has created, and click on the first icon in the Mambosolutions toolbar – 'Insert Head Code'. This will place code similar to below in your document:

> <?php defined("_VALID_MOS") or die("Direct Access to this location is not allowed.");?>
>
> <!DOCTYPE html PUBLIC "-//W3C//DTD XHTML 1.0 Transitional//EN" "http://www.w3.org/TR/xhtml1/DTD/xhtml1-transitional.dtd">
>
> <html xmlns="http://www.w3.org/1999/xhtml">
>
> <head>
>
> <?php if ($my->id) { initEditor(); } ?>
>
> <meta http-equiv="Content-Type" content="text/html;><?php echo _ISO; ?>" />
>
> <?php mosShowHead(); ?>
>
> <?php echo "<link rel=\"stylesheet\" href=\"$GLOBALS[mosConfig_live_site]/templates/$GLOBALS[cur_template]/css/template_css.css\" type=\"text/css\"/>" ; ?><?php echo "<link rel=\"shortcut icon\" href=\"$GLOBALS[mosConfig_live_site]/images/favicon.ico\" />" ; ?>
>
> </head>

Making Your Own Joomla! Template

Now either create or copy/paste your Body content, remembering to close the end Body and HTML tags. Let's assume that you have gone for a simple three column design, leaving a section at the top for banner adverts and a logo, as pictured below.

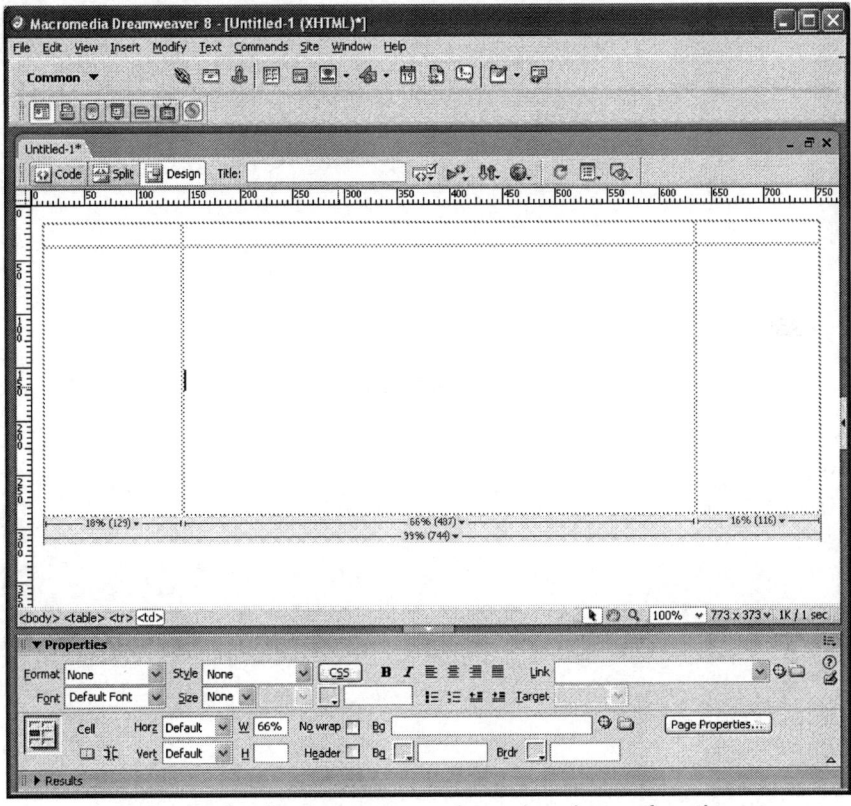

10.2. A simple structure, ready to drop in our functions

Now that we have our structure it is relatively straightforward to add in the various elements into it. Start with the top-middle cell, and click on the Banners icon within the Mambosolutions toolbar. You can tell which is which by hovering over each icon and reading the tooltip. This will insert <?php mosLoadComponent("banners"); ?> into the cell. Next select the top right cell and insert the date. In the left and right columns place the Left Modules and Right Modules respectively. Finally, in the middle column insert the Pathway, press Enter to move down a line and then insert the Main Body content. Take a little time to vertically align the content and you should have a screen looking similar to the one below:

Building a Website Using a CMS in 90 Minutes

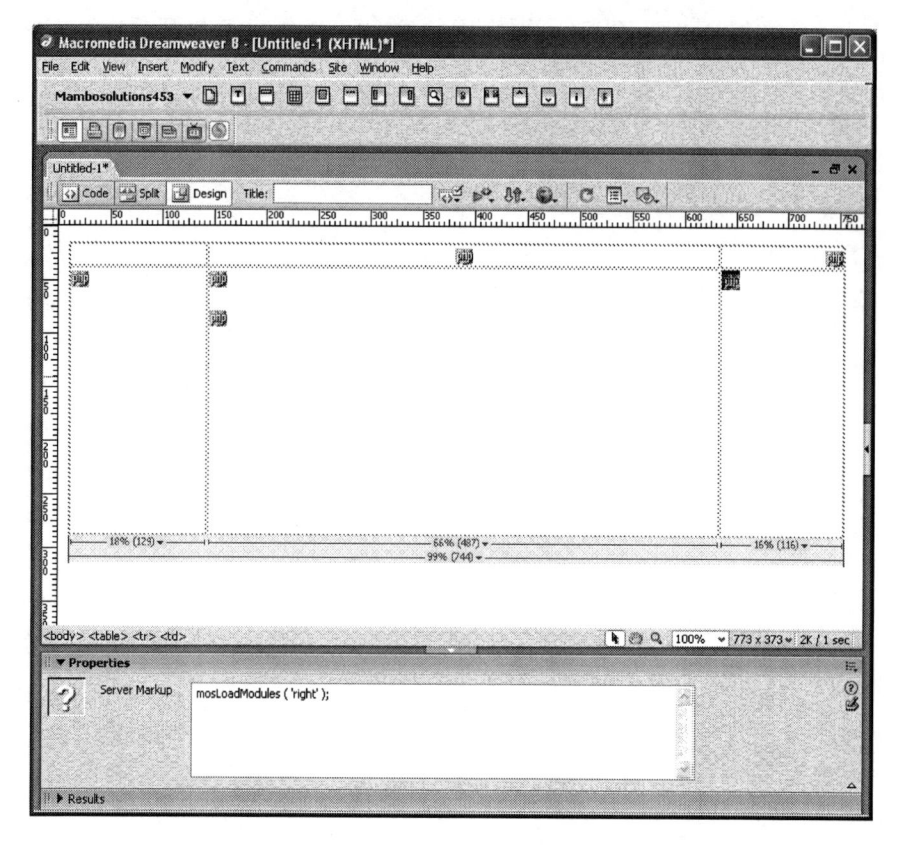

10.3. A template with some of the main modules in place

This example only has a few of the many module positions added, and if you want to design good, well laid out templates, you will spend a great deal of time at this particular stage.

You can also start to add in your graphics. All graphics must be in .gif, .jpg or .png format, and located in an \images folder directly underneath where your index.php file is stored.

Adding CSS to your template

The list of CSS entries for Joomla! is expansive to say the least, with literally several dozen styles that apply to various levels of your template. It can be extremely difficult and time consuming to create a CSS file from scratch, but there are two suggestions you can follow:

1. Copy the CSS from an existing template and then modify it to suit, although be mindful that the template you use may not have CSS listings for every module
2. Download a blank CSS template, an example of which is available at http://livesite.compassdesigns.net/templates/livesite/css/blank css.css and add in CSS styles. Note that this contains an exhaustive list of styles, many of which you may not need

A comprehensive list of styles is provided in Appendix 1.

Once you have created your styles, save the file as template_css.css and place it in a folder beneath the location of your index.php file called \CSS. It is also good practice to validate your CSS, either in Dreamweaver or using an online free validator such as http://jigsaw.w3.org/css-validator/.

Creating the XML file

The last item you need to create is the XML file that Joomla! reads to install your template. This contains several elements:

- **Name** – name of your template, displayed within the administration section
- **Author** – lists you as the author, also displayed alongside the template name
- **Copyright** – allows you to append a date and copyright notice
- **authorEmail** – used to hyperlink your name to your email address from within the template administration section
- **authorURL** – used to display and hyperlink to your web site from within the template administration section
- **version** – displays the template version number
- **description** – allows you to add a longer description to the template
- **files** – used to start the section that lists the location of the index and template_thumbnail.png files
- **images** – used to start the section that lists the location of all images associated with your template
- **css** – used to locate the name and location of your css file

An example template file might look something like this:

```xml
<?xml version="1.0" encoding="iso-8859-1"?>
<mosinstall type="template">
  <name>Demo template</name>
  <creationDate>August 2006</creationDate>
  <author>Martin Bailey</author>
  <copyright>&copy 2006 Martin Bailey </copyright>
  <authorEmail>my@emailaddress.com</authorEmail>
  <authorUrl>http://www.marketingyour.biz</authorUrl>
  <version>1.0</version>
  <description>Demonstration template</description>
  <files>
    <filename>index.php</filename>
    <filename>template_thumbnail.png</filename>
  </files>
  <images>
    <filename>images/ logo.gif</filename>
    <filename>images/bg_grad.gif</filename>
    <filename>images/pic1.gif</filename>
    <filename>images/pic2.gif</filename>
    <filename>images/pic3.gif</filename>
  </images>
  <css>
    <filename>css/template_css.css</filename>
  </css>
</mosinstall>
```

Create this file in Notepad or your favourite XML editor, substitute the information above for your filenames, and save it as templateDetails.xml

Making Your Own Joomla! Template

Wrapping it all up

You now have all of the pieces you need for your template to work. The last stage is very simple. Create a zip file with all of your files in it, ensuring that your index.php, template_thumbnail.png and templateDetails.xml file are all in the root directory, and that you have your \css and \images subfolders correctly created and populated.

In Windows XP, creating this file is easy. Select all of the files and folders, right click over one of them, select Send To, and then Compressed Folder. This will create a zip file with the same name as the file you clicked over, and will place all of your files and folders in it.

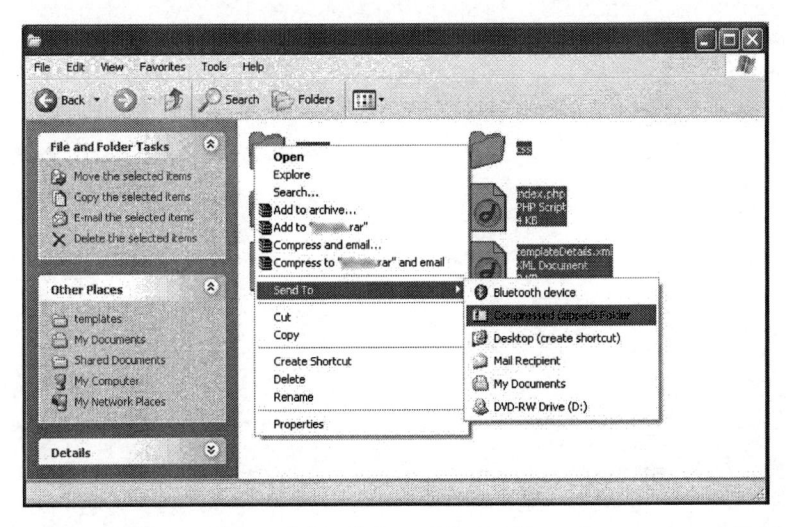

10.4. Select all your files, right click and Send To a Compressed Folder

Testing your template

You are now ready to test your template! You can use the same process to install your template from the zip file you just created as you would with other templates you may have downloaded. Click on Installers, and then 'Templates – Site'. On the following screen click on Browse, select your newly zipped file followed by Upload file & Install.

If you make a mistake in your XML file then this stage is where it is likely to manifest itself first. The most common error is either listing a file that is not available within the zip file, or a typo in the filename/location, which essentially adds up to the same thing – Joomla! cannot find the file within the zip file to install and returns an error. Go back and check all the

75

Building a Website Using a CMS in 90 Minutes

filenames and paths in your XML. Also, connect to your web space, locate the \Templates folder and delete the folder with your template's name beneath it, otherwise you'll get an error next time you upload that the file/folder already exists.

Assuming you've now successfully installed your template you will now be returned to the Template Manager with a listing of the installed templates, which now includes your new one. If you just have one green tick under the Default column, then check the radio button to the left of your template name and click on Default. If, however you also have a green tick under 'Assigned' against another template, tick the radio button and on the next screen unassign any pages by selecting None followed by Save. Once done, click Site, Preview and In new Window to take a look at the fruits of your effort.

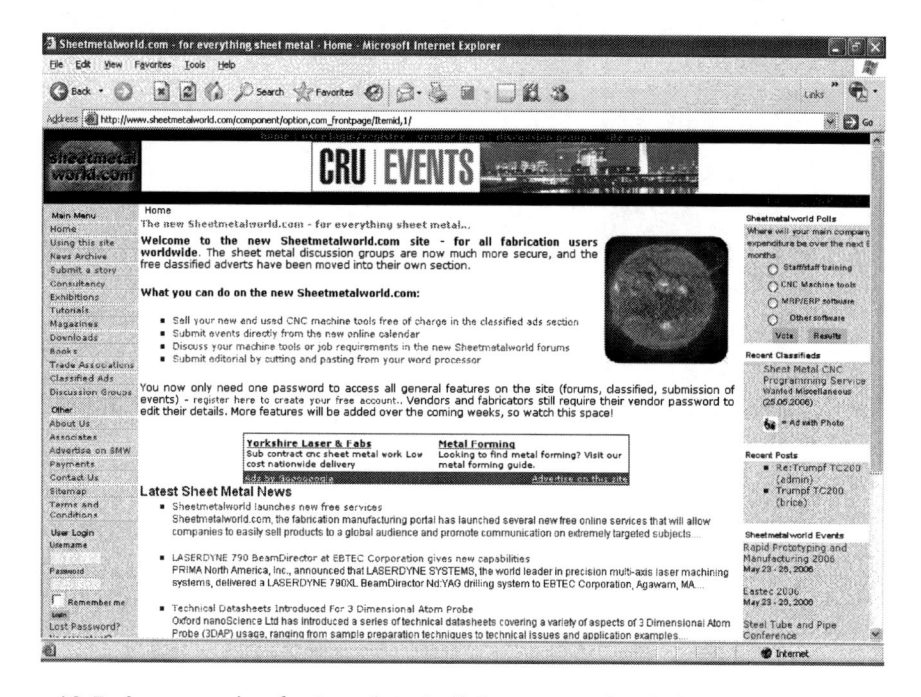

10.5. An example of a template built from scratch, similar in layout to fig 10.3 but with CSS and graphics added

If you are 100% happy with your template at this point then you are obviously a genius! For the rest of us there will be a lot of additional tweaking required after this point, although you will not have to follow the same procedure from here on to re-upload your files. It is possible to edit both your HTML and CSS files within Joomla!, however it is generally easier to edit them in your preferred editor and then upload them via FTP to the relevant location within \Templates\Your Template Name\ folder. Normally most changes will be CSS-related, or by simply adding in more modules that you did not add into the initial index.php template file.

Summary

Designing your own template is only for advanced users with considerable HTML and CSS experience, but those with the appropriate skills can reap the benefits of designing a unique site. It also allows you convert static HTML sites to Joomla!-powered ones, breathing new life and functionality into an existing design. Be prepared for plenty of hours spent tweaking the CSS and HTML once the initial template is installed and operational.

11. Optimising Your Site for Search Engines

Historically, CMSs were notoriously difficult for search engines to categorise. Half the battle related to the web addresses generated for each page. No doubt you've noticed that your web address currently has a rather long string of words and numbers after it, such as:

/index.php?option=com_content&task=blogcategory&id=1&Itemid=3

The problem (for search engines) is that a static HTML page is a physical file that can be found at the same location. Search engines don't like URLs that have 'variables' included, and the above example includes four:

option=com_content

task=blogcategory

id=1

itemid=3

These four pieces of information tell Joomla! what type of page it is loading, how it is supposed to be displayed, and then provide the unique identifiers that point specifically to the content you are trying to view. Search engines don't like variables, and some won't even spider sites where they interpret more than a couple of variables in the URL.

So how can you get around this? Fortunately, both Mambo and Joomla! have the ability to enable 'SEO' – Search Engine Optimisation. This uses what is known as the 'htaccess' file.

What is the .htaccess file?

The htaccess file which, to give it its proper filename is .htaccess, is a text file that controls various aspect of how the web server processes instructions and accesses files. For example, you can specify what error page is displayed, prevent viewing or password-protect a directory and much more, although for this exercise you will not need to do anything more than rename a file – more on that later.

htaccess files affect the directory they are placed in and all sub-directories underneath them. It is important to note that this can be prevented (if, for example, you did not want certain htaccess commands to affect a specific directory) by placing a new htaccess file within the directory you don't want affected with certain changes, and removing the specific command(s) from the new htaccess file that you do not want affecting this directory. In short, the nearest htaccess file to whichever file is being accessed is treated as the htaccess file. If the nearest htaccess file is your global htaccess located in your root, then it affects every single directory in your entire site.

Now that you understand the basics of the htaccess file, let's put it into the context of how it affects Joomla! When placed in the same directory as Joomla! the htaccess file influences every request to load a page that is made to your site. In short, instead of the unwieldy URL we saw earlier you end up with something like:

/component/option,com_contact/Itemid,2/

While this still gives Joomla! the information that it needs to display the right page, search engines do not view these types of URL in the same light as the previous example. You don't need to know how the htaccess file works – you just need to know that it does and how to enable it.

Enabling Search Engine Optimisation

This is a two-stage process. Firstly, log into your administration control panel, click on Site and Configuration, and then SEO. Tick the Yes box for Search Engine Friendly URLs. A dialog box will appear. Click OK, followed by Save.

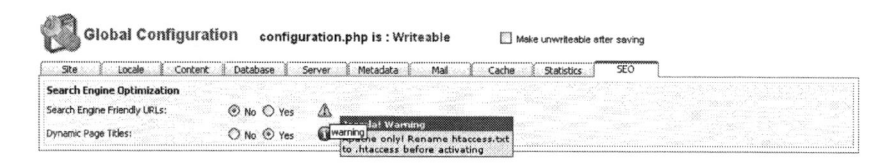

11.1 Enabling Search Engine Optimisation within Joomla!

When you uploaded Joomla!, there was a file called htaccess.txt. The nice guys at Joomla! provided a htaccess file with all of the changes you need so that you don't have to do anything but rename it. Open your FTP software again and connect to your webspace. Locate the htaccess.txt file and rename it to .htaccess – for those who are fairly PC savvy, this will seem different from the usual 'filename.ext' format of having the 'file name dot file extension type' – don't worry, you are reading these instructions correctly!

Once done, revisit your home page and start browsing around. You'll see that your URLs have changed to the new format. If you have a problem at this stage, simply rename the .htaccess file back to htaccess.txt, and switch SEO friendly URLs off from within the administration section. The problem is likely to be a configuration conflict between the instructions within the .htaccess file and that of your server – contact your web host to see if they can assist, asking them specifically if they have any Joomla! or Mambo sites running on their servers and whether they are using SEO-friendly URLs.

Note: There are some modules that may not 100% compatible with sites using Joomla!'s SEO functionality. Before installing a specific module it is good practice to read the developer's support forums and see if anyone is having problems.

Optimising your keywords

Getting Joomla's URL's search engine friendly is only half the battle. Now that search engines can comfortably access your site you need to give them something worth accessing! It is not enough simply to build a site – you need to carefully select chosen words and place them in strategic places within your site. These words are known as 'keywords'.

Search engines work by finding sites that match a user's search criteria. Finding the right keywords to inject into a site is the number one priority for anyone looking to optimise a site for search engines. You may think you know what words and phrases people are using to find sites similar to yours, but you will probably be very surprised by some of the words and phrases people actually use. Thankfully there are several online tools that can help you to select the best words and phrases based on live search data. Of course Google has one such instrument – Sandbox. This free and extremely useful tool is hidden within their Adwords service, but you can access it directly at the following web address:

https://adwords.google.com/select/main?cmd=KeywordSandbox

(If this is not working by the time you read this, do a Google search for 'Google Sandbox').

Start by entering either a keyword or phrase in the box, selecting the relevant language and country and then clicking the submit button. Google will check its databases and give you a list of specific and similar matches. It won't tell you which are the most popular phrases, but there are other ways to find this information out!

You can also try Google's 'AJAX-powered' Suggest, at http://www.google.com/webhp?complete=1&hl=en – this looks like the traditional Google search, but as you type each letter it provides you with possible keywords, along with the number of results – this is useful for seeing the difference between single and plural keywords.

Building a Website Using a CMS in 90 Minutes

Overture provides a similar keyword search service at http://inventory.overture.com (now owned by Yahoo, so this link may change by the time you read this) – entering a keyword will show you the frequency of searches for similar words or phrases for the previous month. This system is great for checking the popularity of terms that are currently in use. Note of course that the more popular a term, the stiffer the competition you'll face. You should use this on all of your terms to gauge their popularity, and then ensure that you optimise your site for the most important ones.

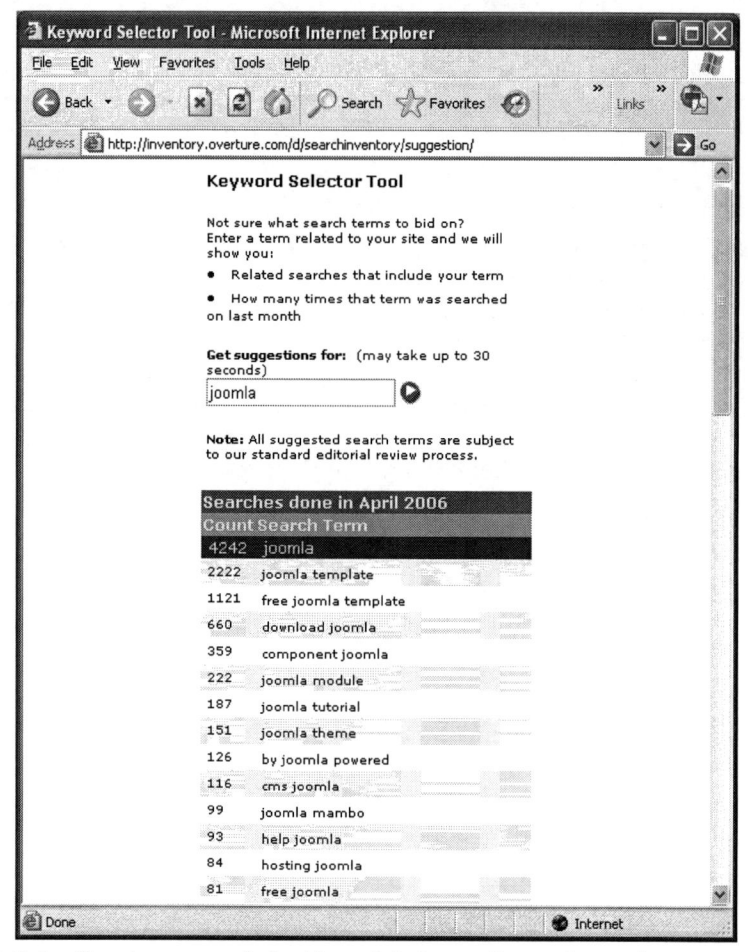

11.2 An Overture search for 'Joomla' shows the various phrases used

If you want to take your keyword accuracy to another level, then it is worth

Optimising Your Site for Search Engines

considering Wordtracker (www.wordtracker.com). This is one of the most widely-used keyword assessment tools online today. Wordtracker works by compiling a database of terms that people search for. You enter keywords on their site and they'll provide you with in-depth analysis of those terms, including:

- How often people use the same words
- Competing sites that use the same words
- Keyword combinations that are relevant to your business
- Your potential for gaining top 10 ranking in major search engines, broken down by search engine
- Identify misspellings of keywords that may be worth optimising for

All of this invaluable data does come at a price, although there is a free 15 keyword trial. Pricing is based on a subscription period, from one day to an annual fee.

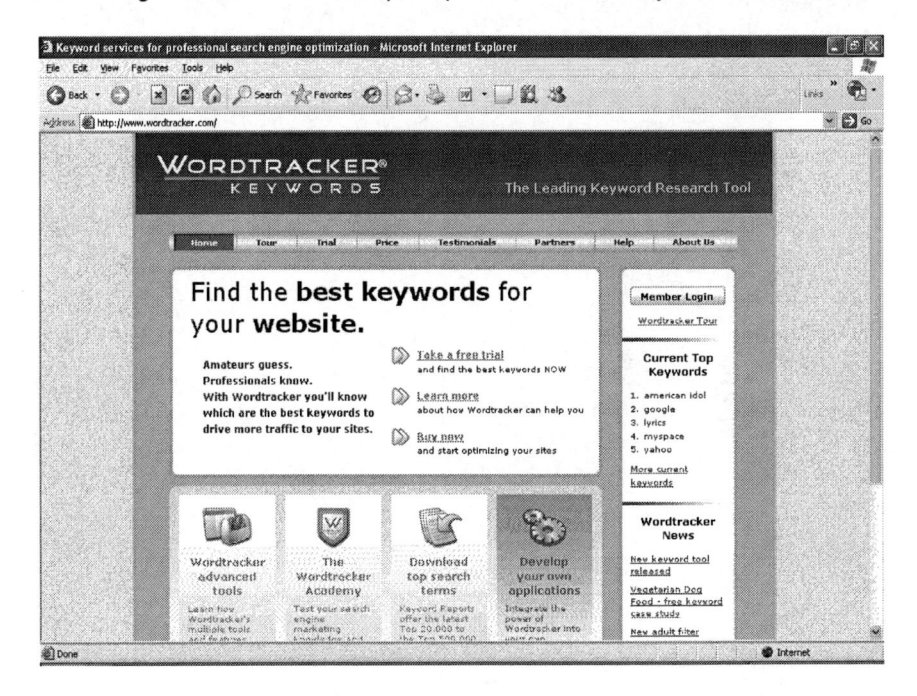

11.3. Wordtracker offers excellent analysis – at a price

When evaluating keywords or phrases, you need to balance the popularity against the competition. Wordtracker helps you do this effectively by suggesting relevant alternatives and then showing you where they are used. In this way you can quickly identify the keywords where you are likely to face less competition.

Building a Website Using a CMS in 90 Minutes

As you dig deeper into the results, Wordtracker also appends a Keyword Effectiveness Index (KEI) number. This measures a keyword's competitive power and is a combination of the number of times it appears across the web against the breadth of sites that it appears on. The trick is to select words that obtain a high KEI rating. Use this in conjunction with other services such as Overture or Google Sandbox to find new keywords and rate their effectiveness.

There are also offline tools that help you analyse keywords on your sites and your competitors. Web CEO is one such tool, and there is a freeware version with a number of features relevant to several sections within this book – more on that later! Download the free version at www.webceo.com, install it and create a free account. Add a new site, go back to the front menu and select 'Research Keywords' and then select the site you just created. You can now either enter some keywords to research or load them from your site. WebCEO will then provide you with the number of daily searches done on your words, the number of competing sites and the KEI.

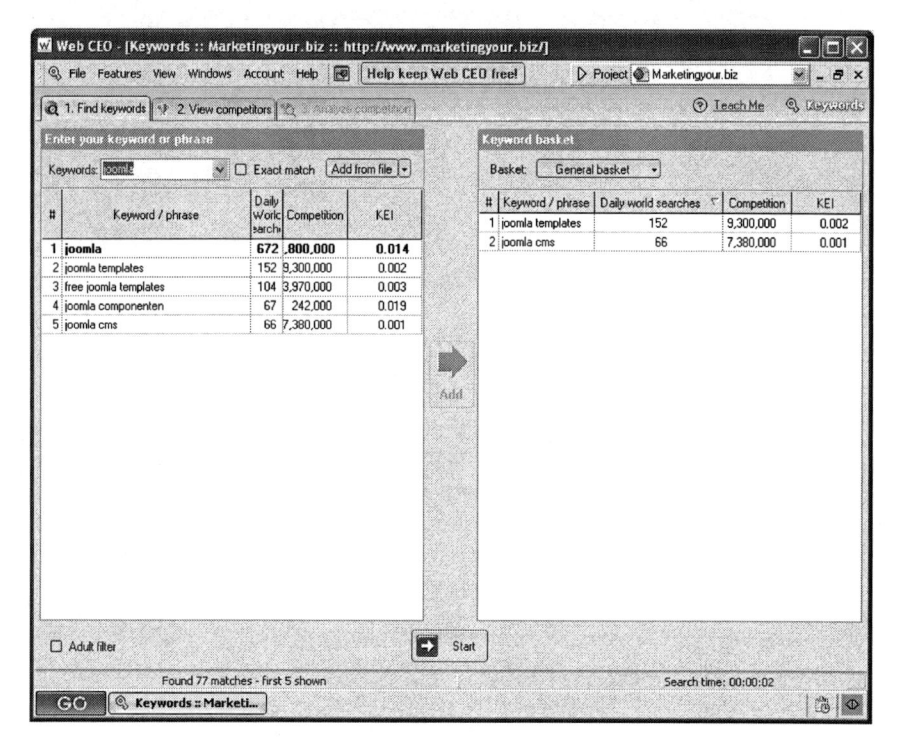

11.4. The excellent (and free) WebCEO can help you analyse keywords

Adding your keywords to the right places within Joomla!

You should now have a better understanding of keywords and their importance within Search Engine Optimisation. You should also have a list of keywords, broken down to the different sections of your site. The next step is to weave these into your content. Thankfully this requires little technical skill from here on in. The first step is to ensure that relevant keywords are placed within the main body of your content. So, for example, if you have a web site related to golfing products, and a specific page on golf tees, then this page would contain the most important keywords or phrases. The title of this page, entered in the Title field of the item details, should also include these keywords at the front of the title. This is especially important as search engines such as Google rank keywords in a page's title very highly.

This alone is not enough – other pages should link to this one using relevant keywords in the hyperlinks. So, for example, you may have a 'Golf Products' link in your main menu, which links to a category containing content pages of relevant items. One content page would be your 'Golf Tees' page – this would be a hyperlink containing 'Golf Tees' which links to a page with 'Golf Tees' in the title and content. Search engines would subsequently see this as a relevant page.

Another good policy is to amend the CSS relating to hyperlinks so that they are bold – search engines rank any highlighting of keyword text as important.

Adding Meta tag information

A Meta tag is a hidden piece of code that is there specifically to tell search engines about your site. Note that adding Meta tags alone is not a magic wand for your site's immediate number one placement, and less importance is placed upon them by search engines than in previous years, but they will assist some search engines in providing additional information about your pages.

Meta tags reside in the <HEAD> area of an HTML page. If you right-click over most web pages in your browser and select 'View Source' you will see that these pieces of code generally appear near the top of the page. The two specific tags you will see on the front page of a 'virgin installation' are:

> *<meta name="description" content="Joomla – the dynamic portal engine and content management system" />*
>
> *<meta name="keywords" content="Joomla, joomla" />*

Building a Website Using a CMS in 90 Minutes

Joomla! allows Meta tags to be added into two main locations within your site:
- At a global level, under Global Configuration\Metadata
- At a content level, for both general and static content

Note: Some other components may also allow Meta data to be associated within pages displayed to the user, or they may automatically be generated by the component. It is worth bearing this in mind, and perhaps checking how the Meta tags appear within specific components by right-clicking over the page and selecting View Source.

Inserting Global Meta tags

From the main menu select Site, followed by Global Configuration and the Metadata tab. In the first field remove the standard text and enter a basic description of your site, remembering to ensure that your most important keyword(s) are present.

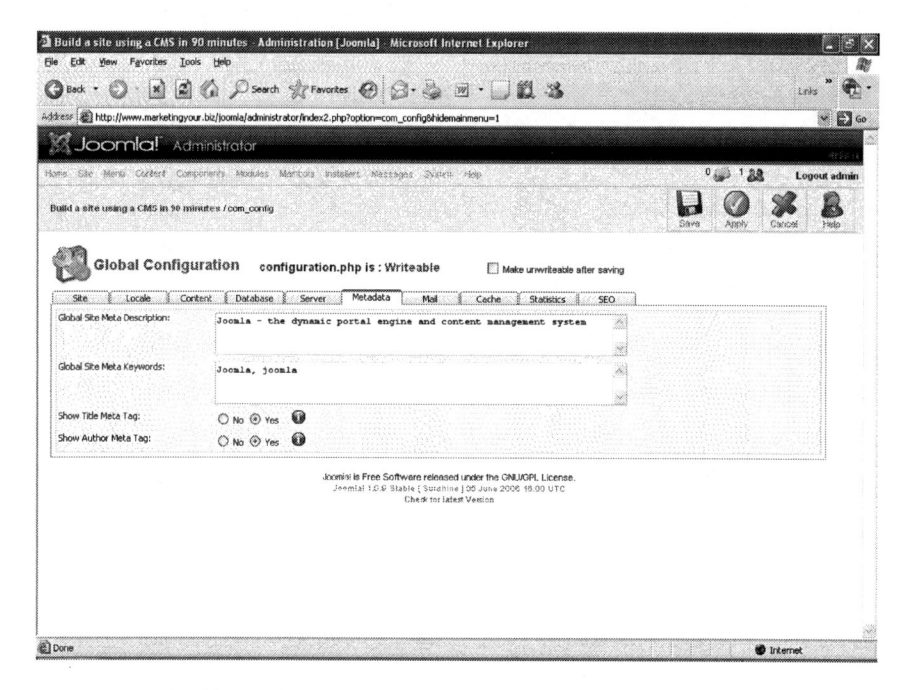

11.5 Modifying Global Metatags within the Configuration section

In the second (keywords) field enter the main keywords that you want to appear on every single page. Note that it is not wise practice to duplicate keywords – while this may accidentally happen if a keyword is added in once in the global settings and once in a content item, ensure that you don't 'keyword stuff' – enter the same keyword several times – as this is frowned upon by search engines.

Leave the two radio boxes underneath set to Yes, which ensures that additional meta tags for title and author are automatically created, based on each content item.

Once you are finished click on Save. If you now preview your site and view the source code you'll see that your Meta tags appear in the <HEAD> section of every page.

Inserting Content Meta tags

Browse to either a category item or static content item and open it. In the tabbed menu select Metadata and you will see two fields similarly titled to the configuration screen. These allow you to add a description and keywords that are relevant to that specific page. Anything you add into these pages is appended after the content inserted by the global Meta tags settings. In other words, what you wrote in the previous section will be included in all pages, and what you add into each content item will be tagged onto the end.

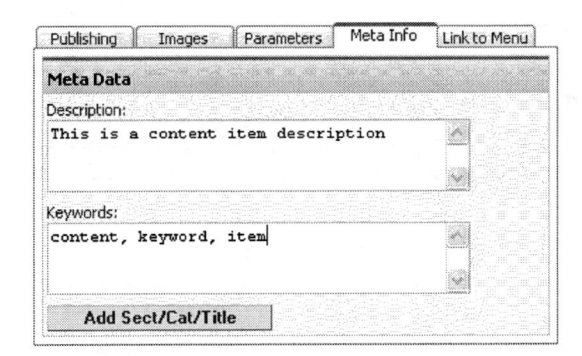

11.6. An example of how content item meta tags can be entered

Now that we have both global and content Meta tags included this is what the resulting code would look like:

<meta name="description" content="Joomla – the dynamic portal engine and content management system, This is a content item description" />

<meta name="keywords" content="Joomla, joomla, content, keyword, item" />

If you've already created other content pages, take a moment to revisit each page and add in relevant keywords, ensuring that they do not duplicate those within the global Metadata section.

Installing a Site Map

The final stage in making your site search-engine friendly also goes a long way to making it more user-friendly as well. A site map is a single page that links to all main and sub-sections. With static HTML sites you have to remember to manually add new sections or pages – not so with Joomla! Downloading and installing the 'Joomap' component (from http://extensions.joomla.org) will automate this process for you – every time a new section, category or content item is added to your site it will immediately appear in your site map without you lifting a finger. It also has the added benefit of automatically creating the Google Sitemap XML-formatted file automatically (see overleaf for more details).

Once downloaded and installed, go to Components, then Joomap. There are three tabbed menu options, although most users will only need the first two. Under Menus ensure that any menus that you are using are ticked, then select Display. By default all of the tick-boxes are checked – modify these settings to suit. Most of these are self-explanatory, however if you are unsure as to what any settings do you can always enable/disable them and see how your sitemap changes.

Next, create your menu link to the Joomap component by clicking Menu, mainmenu, and then New. Select Component, then Joomap from the list of installed components. Type the name as you want it to appear in your menu, then save your changes. Revisit your site and test your site map.

We mentioned earlier that Joomap also creates an XML-formatted output for Google Site Map. This is a free service from the search engine goliath which Google cites as a 'collaborative crawling system allowing you to communicate with Google to keep it informed of changes to your site'. In other words you create a file that is not visible to visitors but that Google can see – this file contains a more detailed site map than a standard one that would appear on your site, detailing new pages and updates to old pages – and all of this is prepared to Google's preferred format. This is especially useful for dynamic sites that Google may have difficulty in spidering.

Optimising Your Site for Search Engines

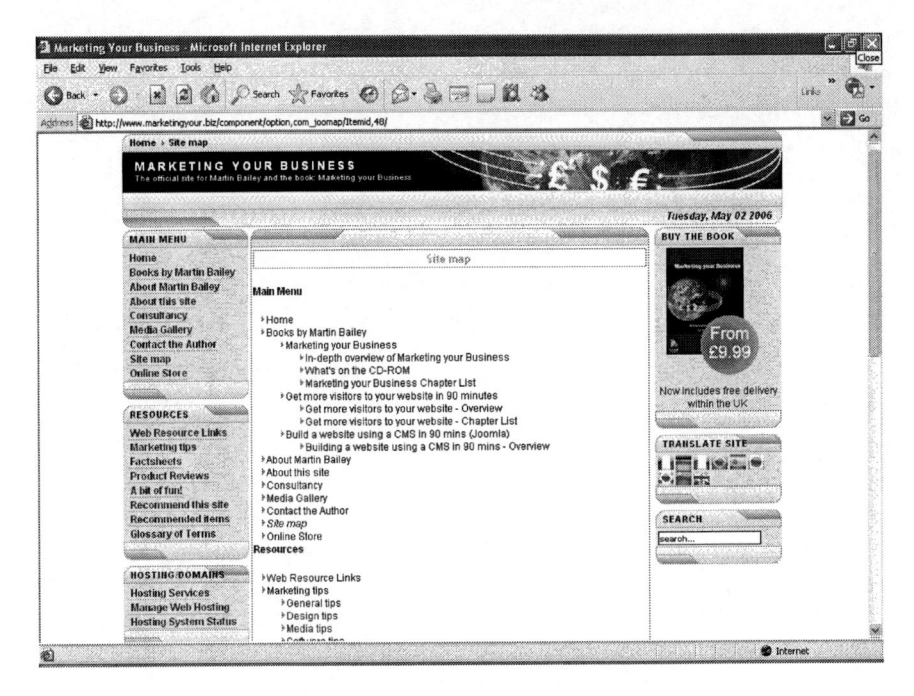

11.7. An example of a Joomap site map

But that's not all! In line with Google's 'do no evil' mantra, they give you something back for providing them with your site information in their preferred format – information. When you log into your Google Site Map control panel you can view information such as:

- Top search keywords used and top keyword clicks
- Status of pages crawled with a list of their PageRank status
- Analysis of content type
- How the site is indexed (e.g. who links to it, who refers to it, similar pages etc)

You need to register at www.google.co.uk/webmasters/sitemaps/ – this is free and if you have a Gmail account you can use that address. You can add as many domains to this account as you want. Once you've registered with Google you will have immediate access to basic information, all of which is actually already available if you know Google's search bar syntax. For example – type site:www.yourdomain.com will show all pages indexed. From within the Site Overview section click on Add a sitemap. Select the

89

type of sitemap (General web) and then click Next. On the next screen copy the URL that can be found within the Joomap Display screen as per the example below, and then paste this into Google Sitemap.

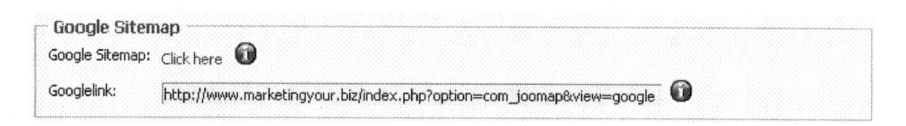

```
Google Sitemap
Google Sitemap:  Click here
Googlelink:      http://www.marketingyour.biz/index.php?option=com_joomap&view=google
```

11.8. The URL of your Google site map, as seen within the Joomap Display screen

Summary

Search engine optimisation is an important step in marketing your site. Get into the habit of adding relevant Metadata to each new page you add. Creating a site map is useful for both search spiders and humans alike. Remember that not all components are 100% compatible with Joomla!'s SEO capabilities, so test, test and retest after enabling. Create a Google Site Map to help get every page on your site spidered.

12. Installing Additional Functionality

What makes Joomla! (and many of the other equally excellent CMSs out there) so great is the abundance of add-ons that are available, often for free. Joomla now has its own 'extensions' web site where you can locate all of the add-ons available. This site is regularly updated and will often feature must-have components, modules and mambots that you'll want to add on your site.

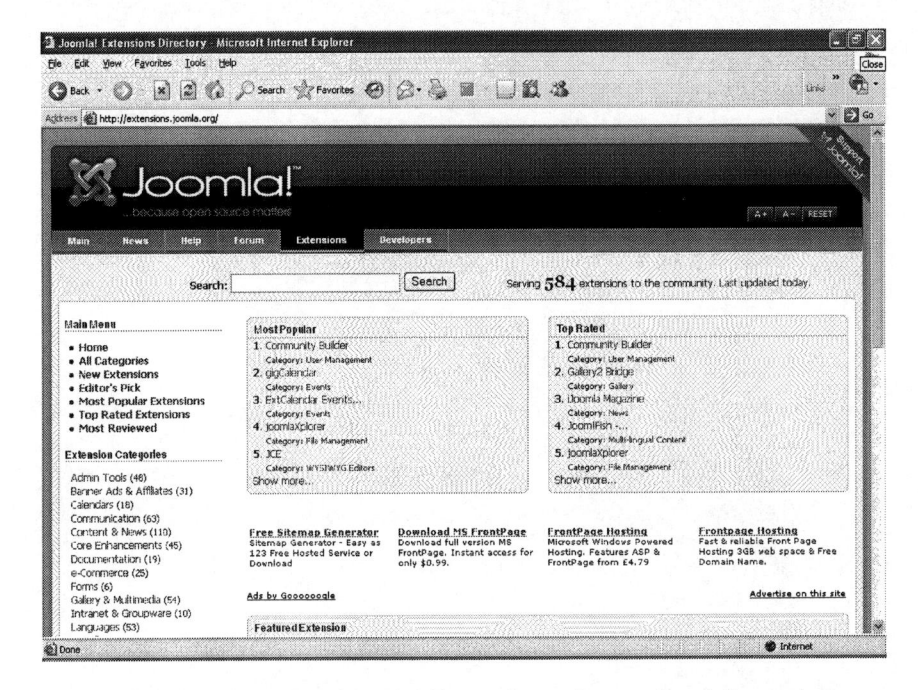

12.1. Bookmark the Joomla! Extensions site, and revisit regularly

Joomla! add-ons come in three different types: Components, Modules and Mambots. We talked about these way back in chapter 4, but will now talk about them in the context of what is available and how you would install/use them. Components are the main 'items', as they generally have modules and mambots associated with them, although you can find separate modules and mambots that each perform specific functions.

Where would you use/see components, modules or mambots?

It is important to understand the difference between these three items, and looking down the list of installed items may help you to do this. From the main menu select Installers followed by Components. Below the Browse/Install buttons you'll see a list of installed components. If you installed the sample data then you'll be able to see these components in action. There are a number of components installed as standard, including a rotational banner engine, mass mail, polls, contacts and web links. Some of these also have their own modules. The screenshot below shows the Newsfeeds component in operation. Essentially, think of a component as providing functionality which will appear in the main content area of your site.

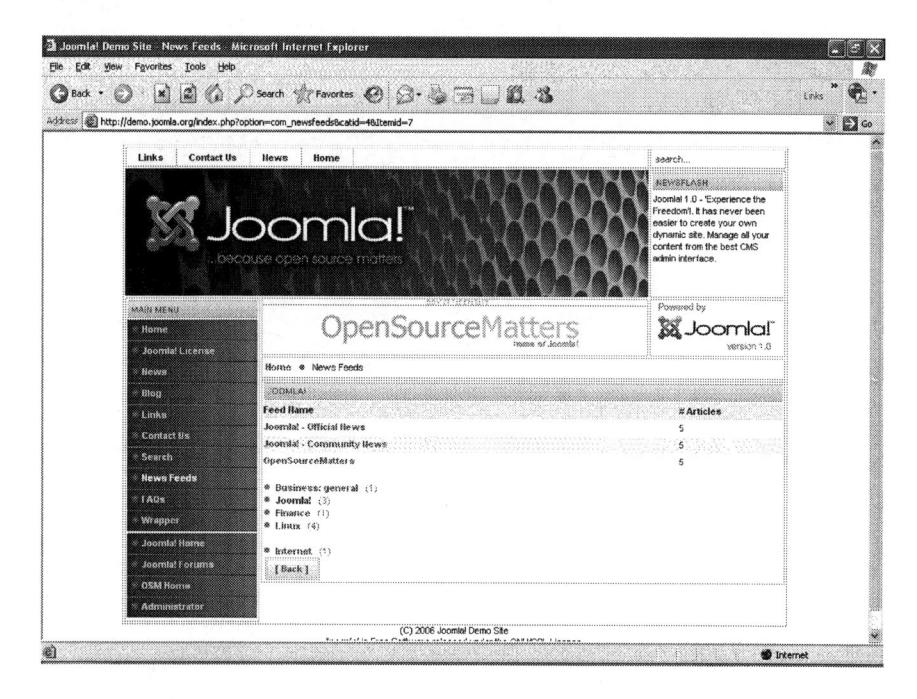

12.2. The Joomla! RSS Newsfeed component

Taking a look at the front page of a test Joomla site will give a good indication of the module's role within your site. Modules are 'blocks' of information that can be placed in specific areas (outside of the main content area) of your site. Cast your mind back to the Templates chapter – when we specified different areas to drop modules into, such as left, right, top, footer, user1 etc. There are standalone modules (such as mainmenu, User Menu

Installing Additional Functionality

and Sections), however invariably when you install a module it will normally be after you installed a component. The front page of a fresh Joomla! install shows several modules in use. To the left we have the main menu, other menu, login form and RSS syndication modules. On the right we can see Polls and Who's online. In other designated areas we have the top menu, search, banner adverts, latest news and popular items.

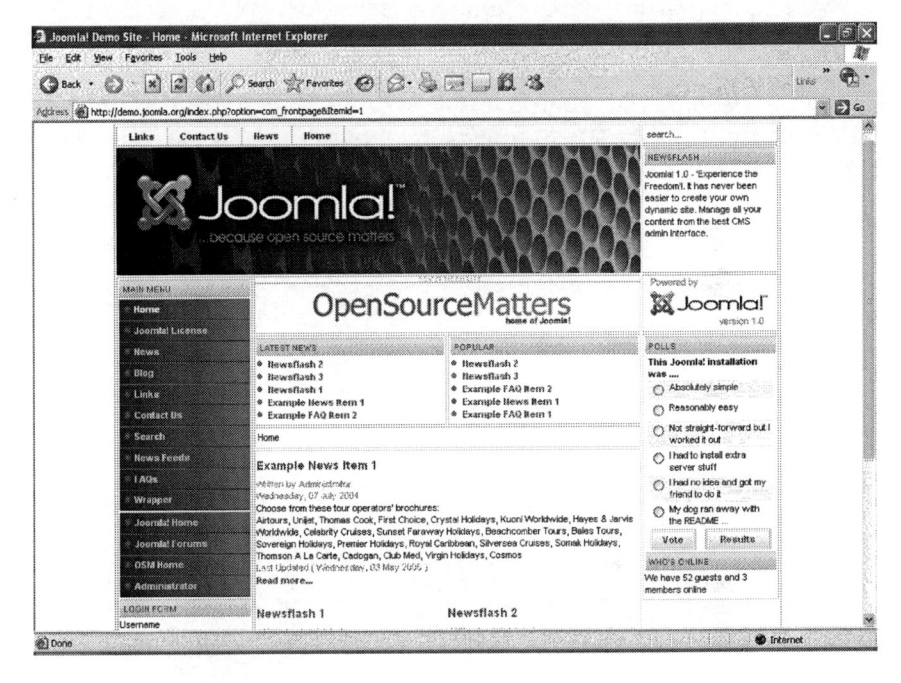

12.3. Various modules in use on the front page.

Mambots are a bit trickier to spot, as their work is mostly done behind the scenes. The best example of mambots in action is the search mambots. To search the content associated with a component, many components will also be supplied with (or have available as a separate download) a search mambot – this piece of additional code tells Joomla! what to search and where to find it. For example, if you download the VirtueMart shopping cart system you can also download a search mambot that will include all of your products in the results of any search that your visitors perform using the standard Joomla! search facility. Another very visible mambot is the WYSIWYG text editor.

Other mambots add functionality that is there for you to use if you know how to use it. It is worthwhile taking a look at each mambot; click on Mambots, followed by Site Mambots to view a list of available mambots. Clicking on a mambot title will give you details on it, the most important of which is the last one – the description. This often gives valuable information about how a mambot is used, or, more specifically what you might need to do to make use of it. Take for example the MOS Pagination mambot – this allows you to break up long pages into two or more. Better still, you can add a title for each page that will appear in an 'Article Index' box at the top of each page, allowing visitors the ability to go straight to the page of interest. All you'd have to do to break up your long document is to add in {mospagebreak title=Your title here} to create a second page with a new title listed in the article index box.

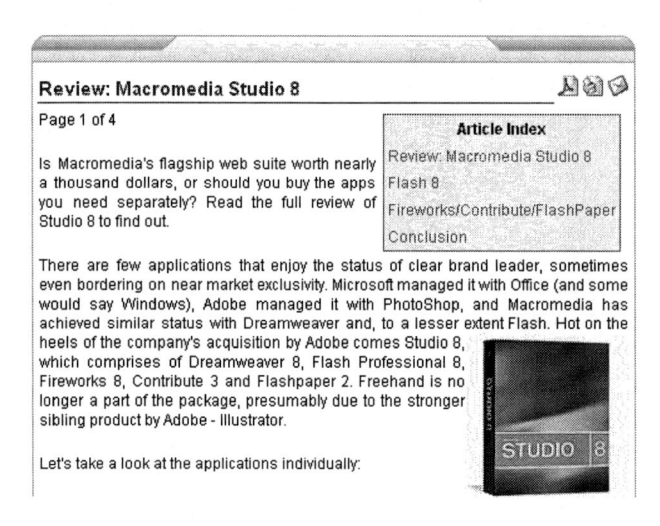

12.4 An example of the MOS Pagination mambot in action

Downloading and installing components, modules or mambots

Components, modules and mambots, like templates, are generally supplied as separate zip files, although sometimes you may be able to download a single zip with all items included. When you visit the Joomla! extensions site and find an item you wish to download, follow the large Download icon.

Installing Additional Functionality

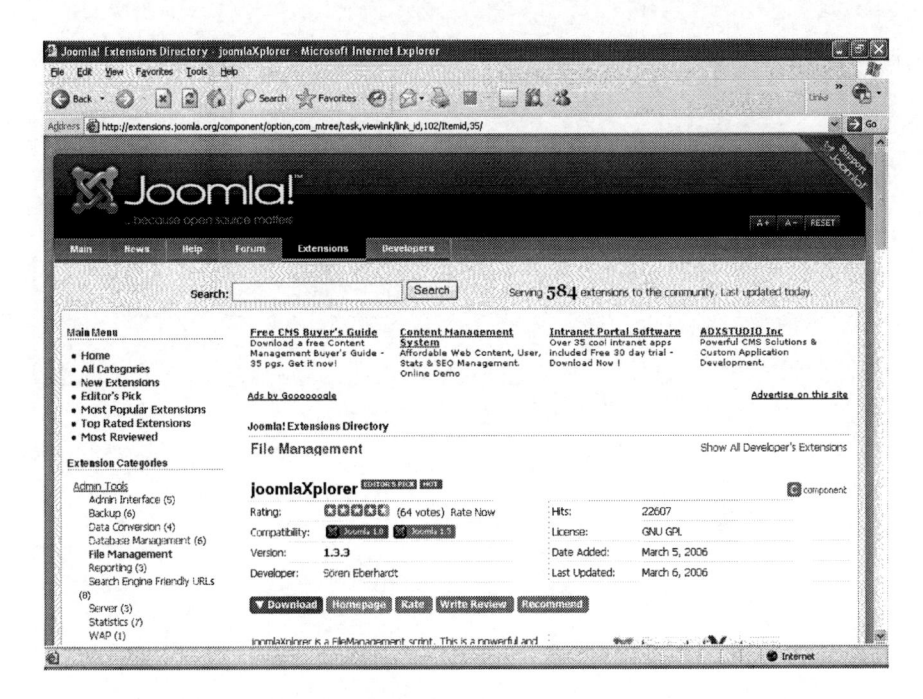

12.5. Follow the download icon on the Joomla! Extensions site

This is where things vary from item to item. The download link will either immediately commence retrieval of your chosen file, or may take you to a different site containing a list of the components, modules and mambots available for this project. Quite often this will be the 'sourceforge.net' site; home to virtually all Open Source projects, although many projects have their own sites, and the link will take you either to the download page or the home page.

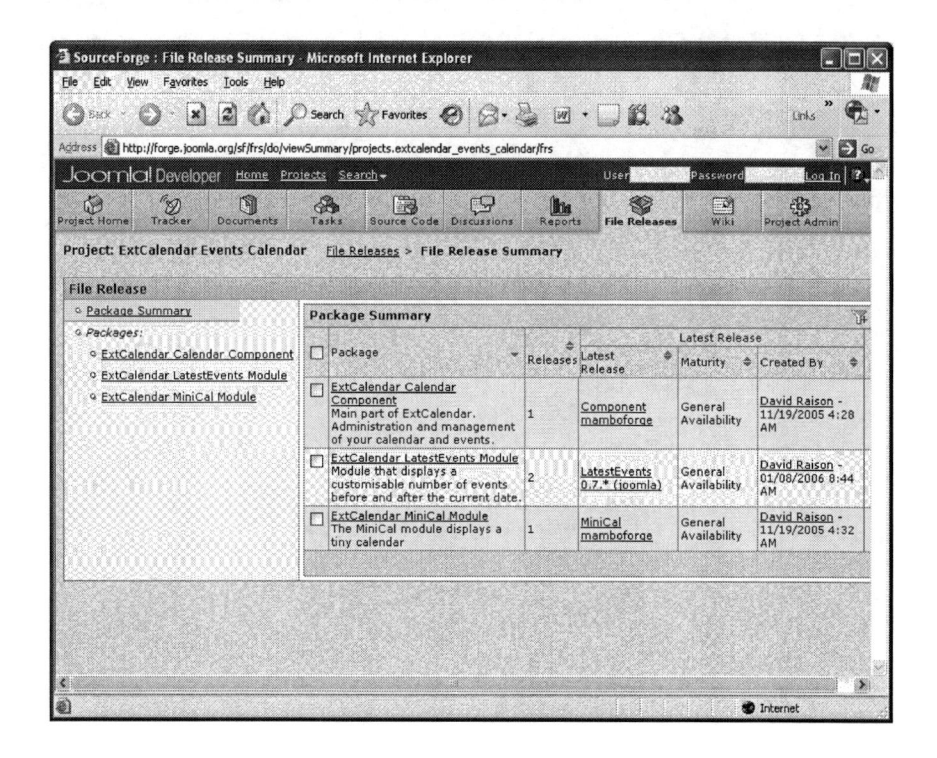

12.6. One project showing the component and two modules, each of which you would download and install separately

To further confuse matters, files are not always provided in the standard ZIP format – they may be .RAR format, amongst others. This does not make any difference to the installation process, as Joomla! can unzip these, assuming that your server supports the GZIP.

The process of installing any of these elements is, as is common with Joomla!, a straightforward affair. Click on Installers, then select the relevant option – Component, Module or Mambot. The next screen is virtually identical for all three – use the Browse button to locate your file, then click on Upload File and Install. Assuming the installation has been successful, you will see a success screen, however this will differ for each installation, as many installers display additional information about the item, its use, where you can donate and how to get support. Some, such as Facile Forms (mentioned further on) require additional processes to be performed, although this is normally only a case of following the on-screen instructions so that the component can be fully installed and configured before use.

Installing Additional Functionality

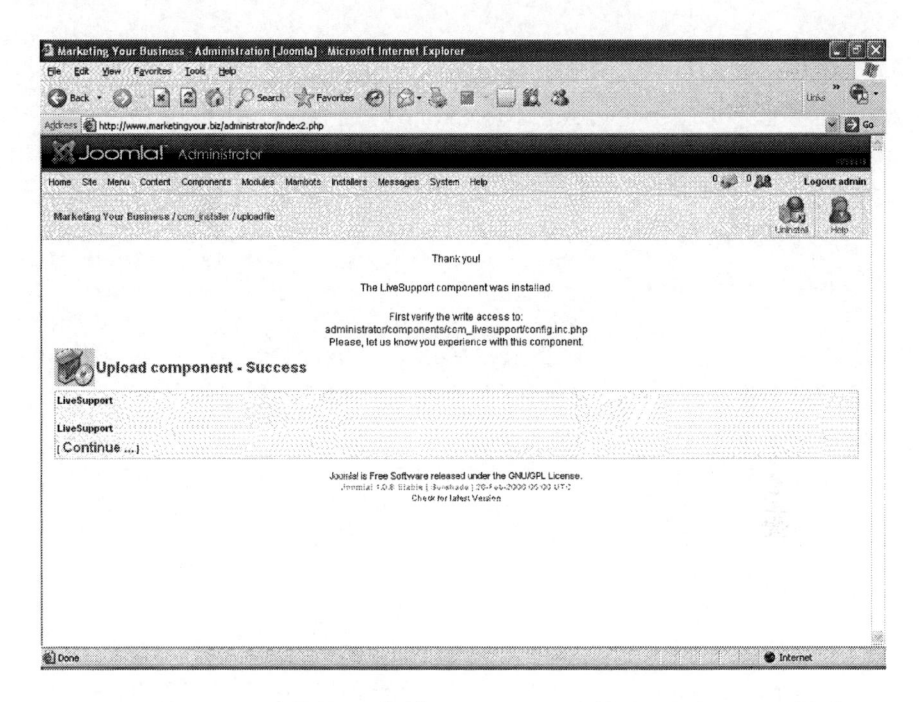

12.7. A successfully installed component, with basic 'success' info

The item that you have just installed will be available for configuration (if applicable) through the relevant menu option. Before you can use them there is an element of configuration required for any/all items:

- Components may need further configuration, or may simply be tools with which to build further functionality – again, Facile Forms allows you to build forms, but the component does nothing immediately after installation unless you build a form
- You will need to add a link to your new component through the relevant menu that you want users to access it from, which will depend on the security access you want to set for it (e.g. registered etc)
- Modules and mambots are installed with the default setting of unpublished – this allows you to configure them before putting them live on your site.

Building a Website Using a CMS in 90 Minutes

What functionality is available?

Let's take a look at some of the most popular components that are available to add functionality to your site. The screenshots below are taken either from www.marketingyour.biz or from the developer's own site. All items are available at http://extensions.joomla.org.

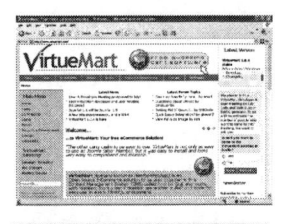

Virtue Mart:
This delivers a powerful and very customisable catalogue and shopping cart facility. Offers wide range of tax rate, shipping rates and payment methods. May be overkill for very small online stores showing only a few products.

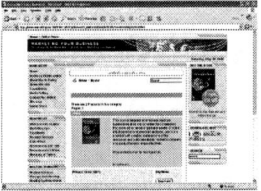

EZ Store:
Much more simplistic shopping cart, which integrates with PayPal. Build your categories and products, add in your PayPal information and your store is ready to go live.

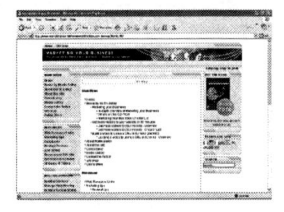

Joomap Site map generator
Automatically generates both a standard site map and Google Site Map file for inclusion in your site. An excellent way to enhance your site in the eyes of both users and Google.

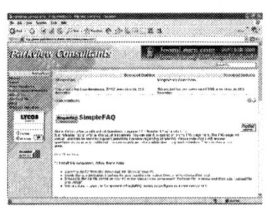

SimpleFAQ Frequently Asked Questions:
Build a knowledge base on your site, broken down into categories. Also allows users to submit their own questions, which only get published after you answer and approve them.

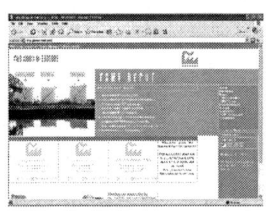

Joomlaboard Forums:
Build your own discussion group. Allows multiple forums, with banned word support, file upload and much more. The only fully integrated solution – most others are standalone systems patched into Joomla!

Installing Additional Functionality

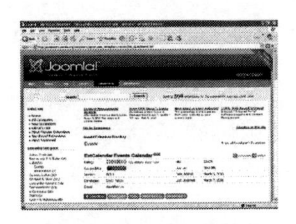

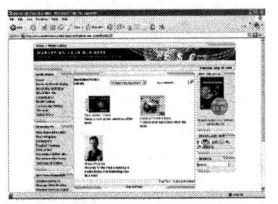

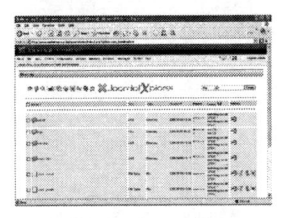

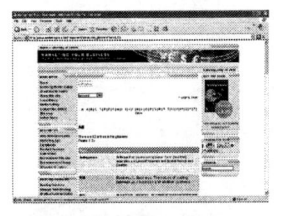

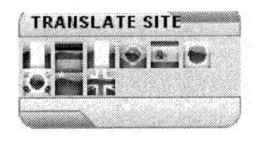

ExtCalendar Events Calendar:
A component and module combination that allows a small calendar (or next events module) to be published, which then links to a full calendar listing. Events can be colour coded and separated by category.

Zoom Image Gallery:
Create different album categories, and then upload your images, which are automatically resized and thumbnailed. Users can create 'lightboxes' to download images, or email images to friends as postcards. Highly configurable.

JoomlaXplorer file manager:
Gives you 'ftp-like' editing capabilities. Easily cut, copy or delete files and folders from anywhere within your webspace (not just where your Joomla! site is located). Useful if you do not have FTP access, but a dangerous tool in the wrong hands!

Glossary:
Component and mambot combination that allows you to add a glossary to your site. The mambot highlights the first instance of a term on any content page of your site and shows the definition in a box when you move the mouse over it.

Classified Adverts
A component and module combination that allows you to display free classified adverts on your site. Registered users can upload images with their adverts. A great way to entice repeat visitors and registered users on your site.

Automatic site translation – G-Tran
This simple module adds eight flags to your site which, when clicked, will use the Google translation engine to translate your site on the fly into French, German, Italian, Portuguese, Spanish, Japanese, Korean, Chinese (simplified) and back to English. You should not rely on this as a 100% translation though – ask any bi-lingual person!

Building a Website Using a CMS in 90 Minutes

Note: If you install, say, ten different extensions on top of Joomla! you would need to revisit the appropriate web site occasionally to check for updates. If a security vulnerability is discovered in a component it is always worthwhile installing the latest version or patch to ensure that your site remains safe. There are normally upgrade instructions on the appropriate site – failing that, subscribe to the site's forum and either read posts from other readers or post a request yourself. The Joomla! community is extremely friendly! Remember to test your components if you install a new release of Joomla!

Summary

The components above give a mere glimpse of the extensions that are available. Visit the Joomla! extensions web site for a complete list, broken down by category. Keep visiting to check for enhanced version or bug fixes. Very often you will get a new version of an extension which can substantially improve the functionality of your site, just by uploading the update.

Pictured below is the extensions menu taken from the Joomla extensions site, showing the breadth of categories.

Extension Categories
Admin Tools (47)
Banner Ads & Affiliates (34)
Calendars (21)
Communication (65)
Content & News (113)
Core Enhancements (47)
Documentation (19)
e-Commerce (25)
Forms (6)
Gallery & Multimedia (53)
Intranet & Groupware (12)
Languages (54)
Miscellaneous (54)
Search & Indexing (36)
Tools (19)
WYSIWYG Editors (6)

13. Multi-lingual Sites

So far we have installed your CMS, added content and functionality and optimised it for search engines. But what if your target market covers more than one language and, more importantly, you have the ability to translate your content, then Joomla! does have the ability to provide a truly multi-lingual site.

A history lesson
With the Mambo CMS system there was a component called Mambelfish. Now we have Joom!fish, an 'official' component (e.g. written by the development team that writes Joomla!) which has been re-written and enhanced.

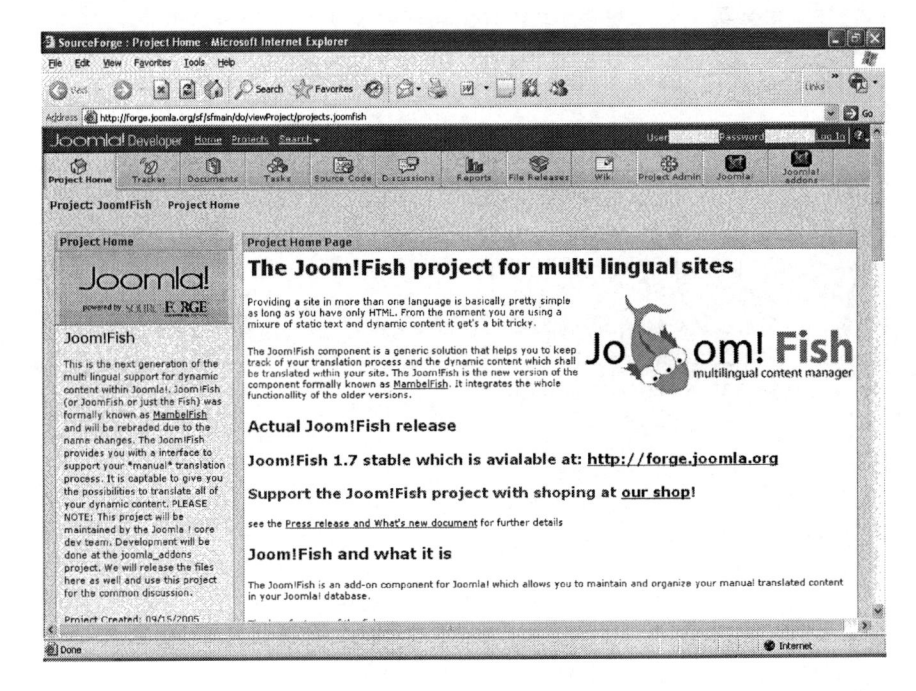

13.1. The Joom!Fish multi-lingual site extension (complete with typo!)

Building a Website Using a CMS in 90 Minutes

With Joom!fish you have the possibility of:

- An unlimited amount of languages
- MANUAL translation of all dynamic content of your Joomla! installation in ONE database
- Overview of the changed contents in the Translation list
- Support for all the core components/modules of Joomla!
- Frontend component for language selection

It is important to stress the fact that this extension is written by the core Joomla! development team. This means that most people that develop additional extensions will strive to ensure that they are fully compatible with multi-lingual sites. As a result you will be able to find a number of files on the Joom!fish web site relating to other extensions that provide better support. There are, of course, no guarantees that some of the more obscure extensions will have full or even any support for Joom!fish, so if there is a function that you need that must be multi-lingual, check it out first before you get too far down the road of installation and use.

Installing Joom!fish

As with all Joomla! installations, this is a simple case of downloading the component from the official site and using the standard installation routine to add it to your site. Once installed you'll see the 'success' page, which does provide some very useful information – if you are new to Joom!fish it would be wise to study it! (If you want to get back to this page, click on Components, Joom!Fish and About, then follow the link on the right to documentation.)

Unusually, the installation routine also installs a range of modules and mambots that are required by Joomla! at the same time as the component.

The next stage is to download and install your language packs – these translate the 'wraparound' languages of the front end of the

13.2. Joom!Fish Content Manager

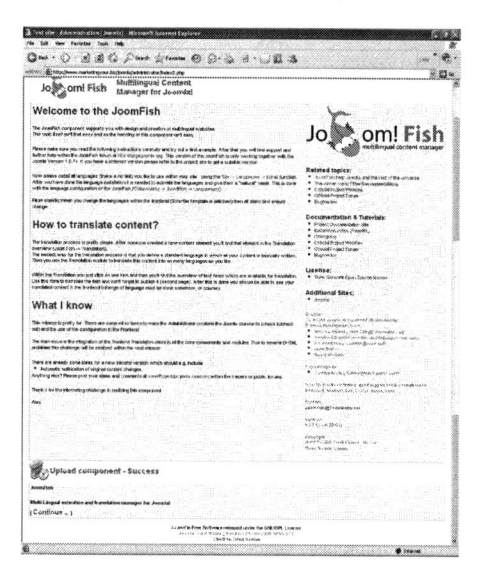

Multi-lingual Sites

site such as menus, module titles, module text etc. At the time of writing, there are almost 50 different languages available – from Arabic to Vietnamese. These are all available from the Joomla! extensions web site.

Now click on Installers and Languages. Browse to your downloaded language zip file and install in the usual way. DO NOT enable the language from the resulting screen as this simply switches between your languages – at this stage there is no option for users to switch languages.

The next step is to configure the overall preferences of Joom!fish. Go to Components, Joom!fish, then Configuration. You can choose the language of the back-end administration interface – 8 are installed as standard. It is also possible to tell Joomla! what to display when a content item has not been translated – you can choose between displaying the original (language) content, showing a default message (along the lines of 'sorry, this item is not available in the language selected') or the original text with information relating to its language. Lastly, you can specify whether users can publish translated content from the frontend.

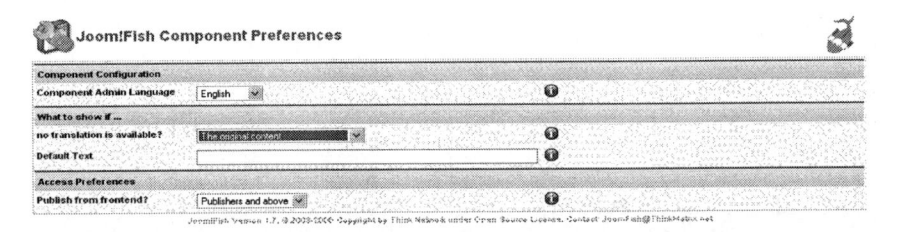

13.3. The Joom!fish configuration screen

Save your changes and then go into the Joom!fish Languages menu option. This is where you enable the various languages for your site. If you just installed the one language pack you'll see two rows – one with English and one with your newly installed language pack. Check the tickbox to the right of your language title. You will also need to enter the official ISO country code for your language e.g. en for English, it for Italian, fr for France etc. The Joomla! filename is usually completed for you, and the image filename can be left blank. Once you are done click Save.

Building a Website Using a CMS in 90 Minutes

13.4. Activating a language just takes a click and the adding of the country code.

We mentioned earlier that Joom!fish installs additional modules and components. These may already be live on your site, however this depends on whether your template has a region that Joom!fish allocates to the module by default – user3. If not, don't worry – as with any component you can position it anywhere within your site. Click Modules, Site Modules and select the Joom!fish language module, then configure as desired.

Now comes the time-consuming part – translating your content! While a great deal of the core language elements will already have been translated you still have a lengthy task ahead of you – especially if you already have a lot of content.

Start by clicking Components, Joom!fish, then Translation. On the right-hand side of the screen you'll see a dropdown menu marked Content Elements – select this and choose one of the options – for this example we'll choose Menus. Select one of the options to translate and you will be prompted with the following screen:

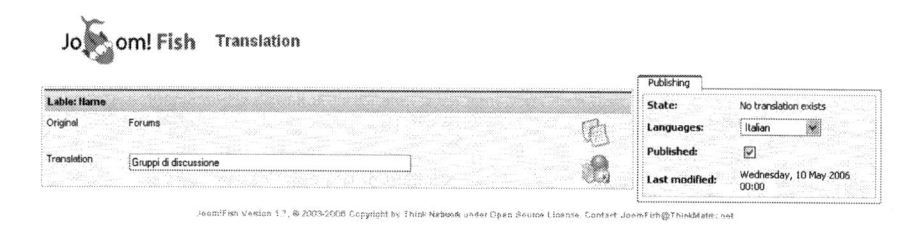

13.5. Translating a menu item involves the translation field, selecting the language and publishing it

Translation is simple – enter the translation in the field below the English text. Next, select your language from the dropdown menu, check the Publish

Multi-lingual Sites

tickbox, then click Save. You'll be directed back to the list of items within your chosen content section.

Original title	Languages	Translation	Last modified	State	Published
Contacts	Italian	Contatti	Wednesday, 10 May 2006 23:09	✔	✓
Forums	Italian	Gruppi di discussione	Wednesday, 10 May 2006 23:18	✔	✓
Home	(no translation)			●	✘
Site map	(no translation)			●	✘
Test menu	(no translation)			●	✘
Web links	(no translation)			●	✘

13.6. The above list shows two items translated into Italian

If you now preview your site, you will see the Language selector in your specified location. It can be formatted as text links, flag links or a drop-down menu. Select your new language and you will then see your translated menu options! No doubt because you are heady with the excitement of seeing your site automatically translate an item into another language, you'll go back to translating the rest of it with renewed vigour!

The first example was the most simple of translation. Most other items that you'll translate will be just as simplistic, requiring a single word or short phrase. Content items are the most time-consuming to translate. For each content item you will need to translate the title, intro text, main text, any image 'alt' text and metadata (keywords and description).

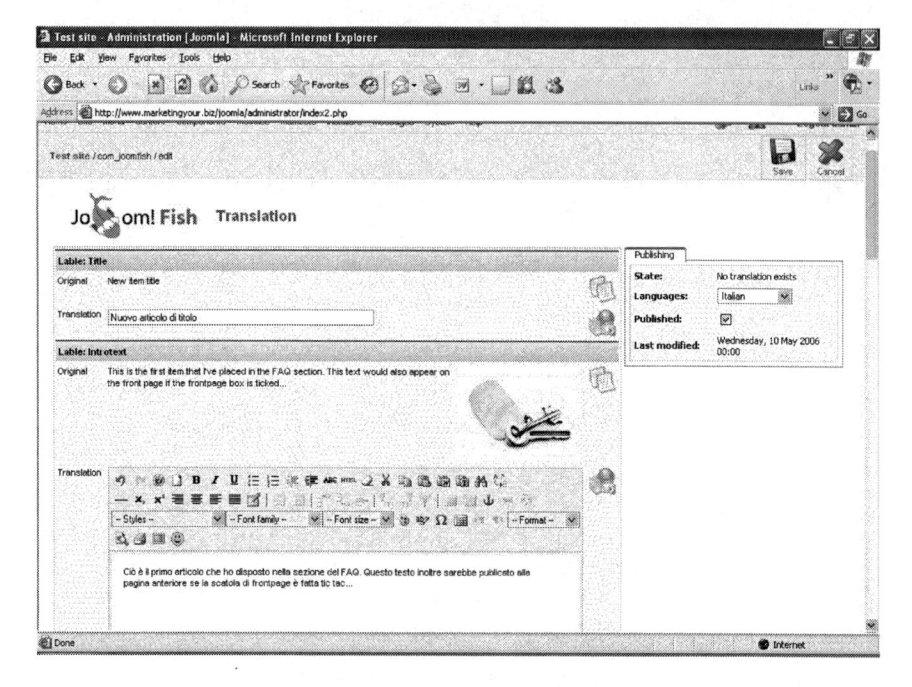

13.7. Translating a content item requires the title intro text, full text and image/metadata to be translated.

You can of course choose to have the majority of the site in one language, with basic content available in other languages. Going back into configuration and selecting the default text to show when an item is not available in the chosen language.

While the translation menu will cover the majority of your site it will not cover many external extensions, although as previously mentioned most of these will have support for Joom!fish. All you need to do is locate the support files (in XML format) from the Joom!fish project site for your extension (or, if not here check the extensions homepage), and then upload these files to the Joomla! administrator\components\com_joomfish\contentelements\sub directory. They will then appear within the translation page for you to translate. This procedure is well documented on the Joom!fish site.

Summary

Joom!fish provides a truly flexible way of empowering multi-lingual site. Once the bulk of the translation has been performed, and all required extensions are installed the workload is much more manageable. Be mindful that some extensions may have limited or no support, although experienced Joomla! users will be able to create the required XML files to facilitate translation.

14. Backing-up Your Site

Although most hosts offer a reliable, robust service, accidents can happen – files can be overwritten or deleted in error and ISPs can go out of business, leaving you high and dry. So what do you do when the worst case scenario occurs? Being prepared is obviously your best defence, so you should take regular backups of your site.

A Joomla! site is not, however, like a standard web site. With static HTML sites, it is just a case of downloading the site to back it up. Joomla! consists of two elements – the PHP scripts (HTML files) and the mySQL database itself. Both items have to be backed up in order for you to be able to restore the site on a new server.

Backing up your mySQL database
The method you choose here will depend on your technical expertise and your web host. The options available to you may include:

- An option within your web-host's control panel to back up your databases
- Access to the popular phpMyAdmin database manipulation tool
- One of several Joomla! extensions that will extract your data and save it as a file on your web server, ready for download via ftp

As the first option is ISP dependent (and will therefore differ between each ISP), we'll move straight onto the second – phpMyAdmin. This is yet another Open Source application which is often installed as standard. If you do not have access to this, then it is available from www.phpmyadmin.net. Many ISPs will have phpMyAdmin installed as standard with any purchased mySQL services.

Warning: This does require a basic understanding of database structures and SQL syntax. If this is a new area, you may wish to skip to the Joomla! backup component section.

Using phpMyAdmin to back up your SQL
phpMyAdmin could almost be described as a browser-based version of Microsoft Access, although the interface is entirely different (and this is not a Microsoft product!). It allows you to create databases (subject to your server's/ISP's configuration), create tables and add/amend data within them. You can also import and export data quite easily, which is what we're interested in here.

If you do not have phpMyAdmin installed then download the latest version and follow the installation instructions – it mainly involves modifying some details in the config.inc.php file, which your ISP can provide if you don't already have them. Once installed you will need to log in using the username and password you specified during the setup process, after which you will be presented with the main administration screen.

Note: Some ISPs will only provide one or a few databases, whereas others will allow many more. You may need to select a database name from the left-hand pane before seeing a list of tables within that database.

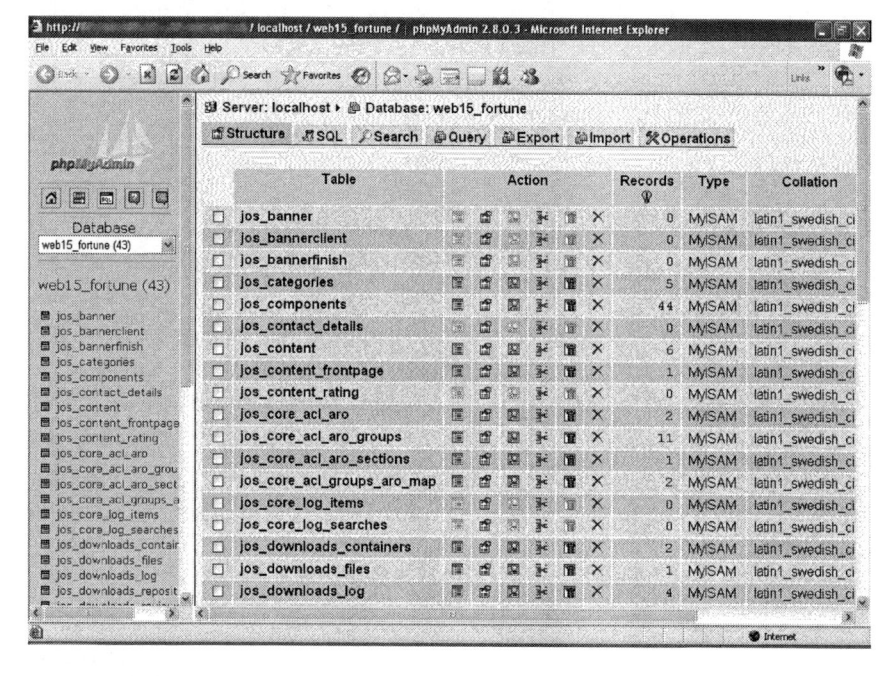

14.1. phpMyAdmin's interface showing a list of standard Joomla! tables

In the example above the database name is 'web15-fortune' – click on this to select the database, and then click on Export.

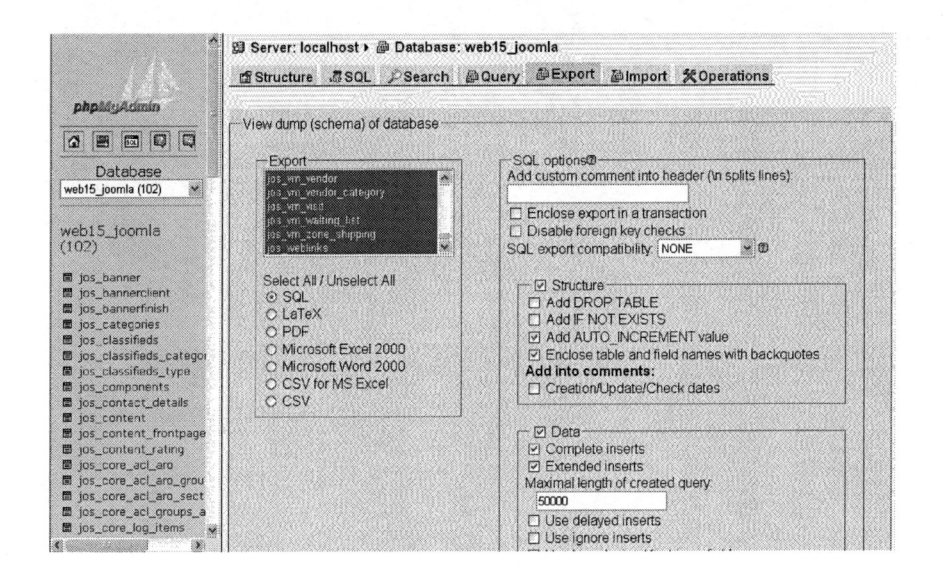

14.2. Selecting all tables for export

Click on Select all to select all of the tables, and leave SQL ticked. Now scroll down, check the Save As tick box, tick Zipped followed by Go. You will then be prompted to Open/Save a zip file – this is your database. Save this to your hard disc, unzip it and open the file in WordPad (not Notepad as it will not lay the contents out correctly).

Note: By using the Select All function you are choosing to export the routine that will allow you to create and populate all of the tables, however this will not create the actual database name itself. This is not a problem, as a) many ISPs don't allow you to create databases using an import into phpMyAdmin and b) in a crisis situation or server move you would manually create the database name and then run the import routine using this file without having to modify it. If you did export the database creation routine as well, don't worry, as you would be prompted with an error when you try to import it – all you have to do is cut out the few lines that refer to the database name near the top of the file. Think of it like a directory structure, with the database name being the top folder, and all tables being the next level. If you manually create (or have created for you) the database name and then just back up the tables, this removes the possibility of problems later when you try to restore.

Building a Website Using a CMS in 90 Minutes

14.3. A sample of an exported mySQL database

On a standard installation, all Joomla! tables will begin with jos_ – in this example you can see the code for creating the jos_banner table, which would contain information relating to the banner rotation component.

The zip file you just created is a simple text file which contains 'SQL' commands that will create all the tables and then insert the data in them. If, for example you had a server crash which resulted in a loss of your database, all you would need to do is create the database name and then select it in phpMyAdmin, click on Import, browse to your SQL file and upload it – your entire database will immediately be restored!

While using phpMyAdmin may appear like a substantial break away from the ease of Joomla!, for the more advanced user it also provides the opportunity to edit some content that may not be accessible through the Joomla! administration section.

Joomla! backup components

If the thought of using phpMyAdmin leaves your blood running cold, and you simply want to have a backup which you can pass to an expert to restore should the worst happen, then you are in luck, as there are of course several

Backing-up Your Site

components that will perform the above, all of which are available on the Joomla! extensions site. The one we shall focus on is eBackup, which provides a comprehensive solution with the configuration options that most will need without being complicated.

To start using eBackup, download it from the Joomla! extensions site and install it using the Components Installers option. Open the administration screen of the component using Components\eBackup from the main menu. You are now presented with a list of all of the tables within your mySQL database (which may contain non-Joomla! tables if you have other applications installed using the same database).

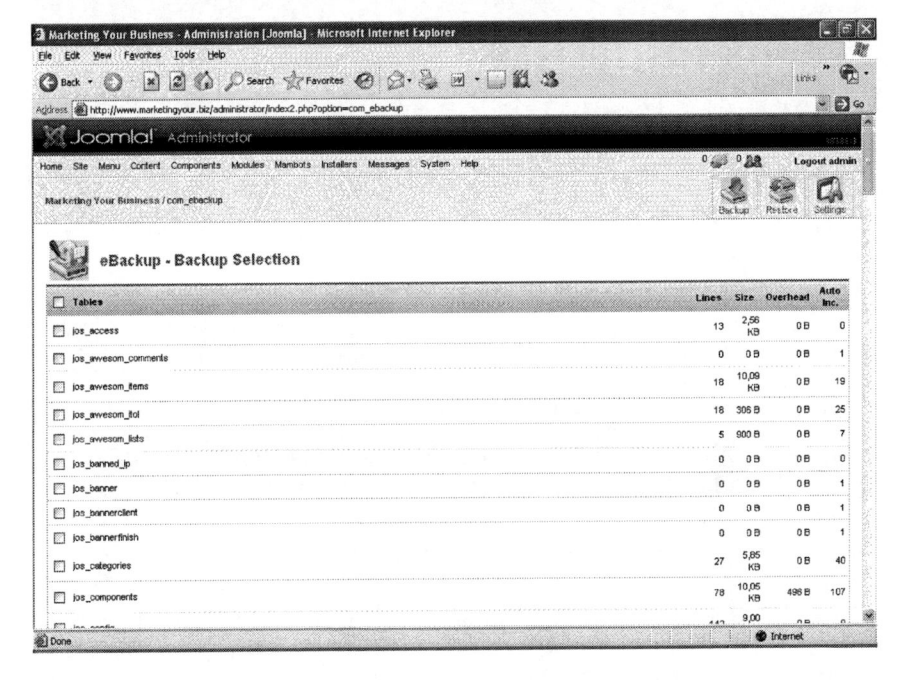

14.4. Your tables, as displayed in eBackup

From here you are two clicks away from completing your task! Click on the checkbox at the top left of your table list (next to Tables) – this will select all of the tables underneath. Now click on Backup and wait – it may take several seconds to back up your database, especially if there is a lot of content. Once it has been completed you'll be taken to a confirmation screen, detailing the file size, name, number of tables and time taken to back up your data. Your file will be stored in \administrator\backups\.

Building a Website Using a CMS in 90 Minutes

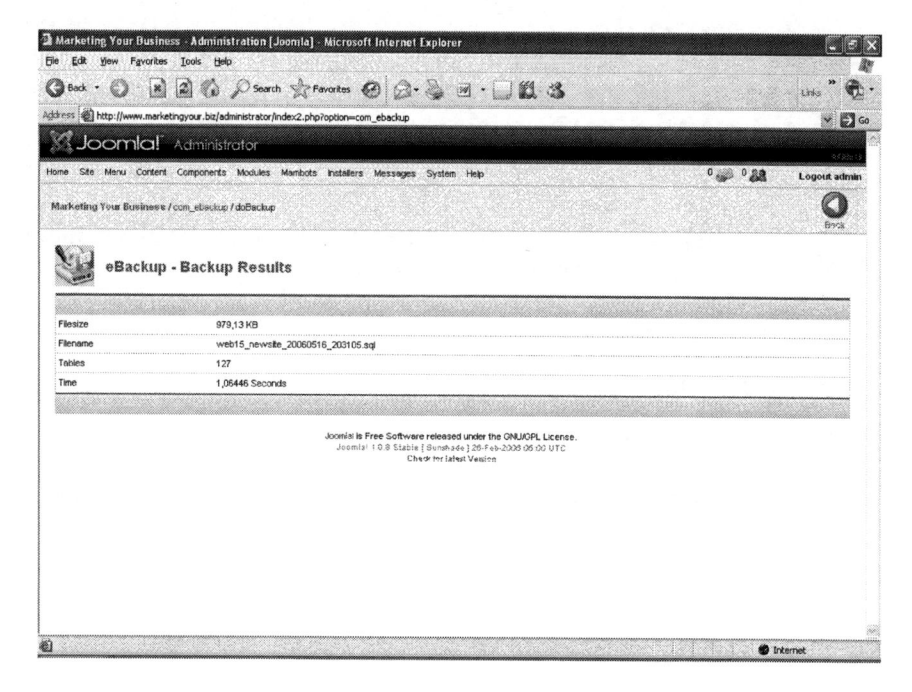

14.5. Your database is now safely backed up

Backing up your HTML (PHP) files

Now that your SQL database is backed up, the next stage is to back up the physical files that make up the site. Your ISP may provide a 'backup and download/email' facility. This will zip up all of the files within your site and then either immediately initiate a download or send the zip file as an attachment on an email. A download is the better option, as many ISPs have a limit on the size of email attachments, and a zipped Joomla! site will start at over 2MB – and that's without all of the extension you install and any graphics you will have uploaded to your site.

Your next option is to use FTP software to download your files. As you've already used FTP to upload your files, it is simply a case of creating a backup folder on your PC, connecting to your web space, selecting all of your files and then instigating a download. Some FTP programs have a synchronise facility, which will drastically speed up subsequent backups as it will only download files that have changed since the last download.

Backing-up Your Site

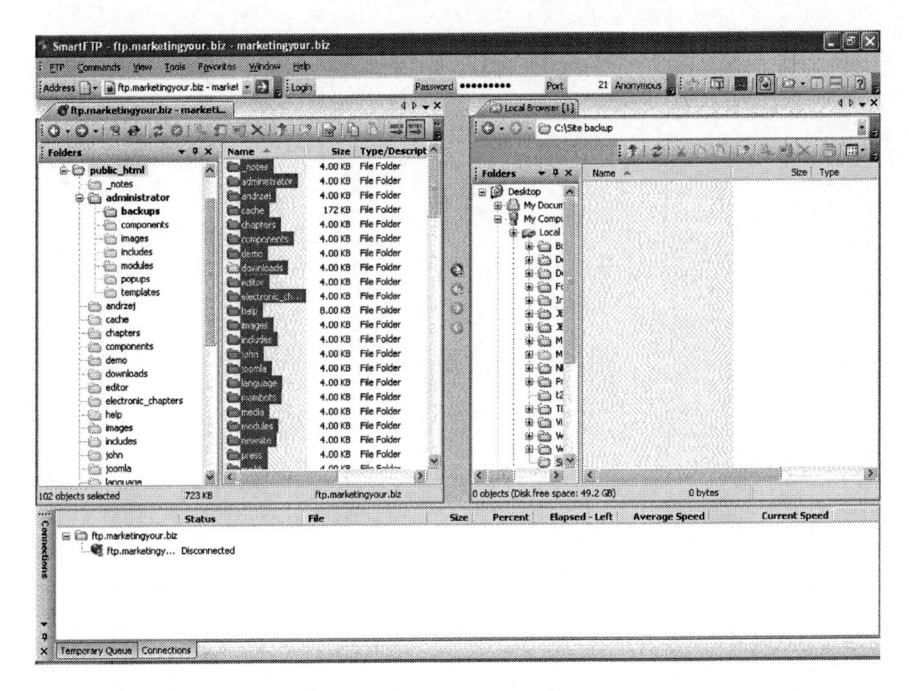

14.6. Drag and drop your site to your hard drive with FTP software

Summary
Backing up your site is one of the most critical but overlooked tasks of many webmasters. Once set up, this two-step procedure of backing up your database and your web files need not take up much time at all, but can be the difference between a quick recovery after a site crash and losing everything!

Summary

- With what you now know about CMS systems, it is quite conceivable to get an idea for a site, buy a domain, upload your chosen CMS system, run the installation routine and start adding in content within an hour. In fact, I've got a core site and components installed in under 20 minutes!

- The functionality, ease of use and availability of extensions will vary considerably between CMS systems. Some continue to flourish while others fade into obscurity. The opensourcecms.com web site is an invaluable resource for testing the usability of the core CMS features.

- When evaluating a CMS, you must consider your end goal for your project.
    - Are the extensions available that you will need
    - Are they well supported
    - Has the CMS been developed for some time, with a healthy number of people developing for it
    - Is it secure? Read release notes to see how often security patches are released and the severity of the problems that they fixed.

  Read the forums of your chosen CMS to gauge users' opinion.

- Finding the right ISP is as important as finding the right CMS. Some will not support a CMS, either partially or completely. Check with the ISP whether they have any configuration problems with CMS systems, and check their support forums to read other's opinions if possible.

Moving forward

Once you have your site up and running, with your extensions installed and with content being added (either on your own or with the collaboration of others) you may be happy to just add content within the existing framework. Maybe for you the CMS is just a means of easily adding or amending site content, which is fine. But for those looking to constantly add new features to their site, the unending flow of new and updated extensions available from developers all around the world will constantly open new doors. You may even stumble upon an idea for a new extension that could benefit you and others – with PHP and mySQL so widely supported it is easily to locate developers that can help if this is not a skill-set you possess.

- Keep visiting your CMS source site (e.g. Joomla.org) for new versions and security releases, but be mindful that installing a main Joomla!

update may stop older extensions from functioning. It is therefore important to test your site thoroughly after installing any updates, and back up your database and scripts regularly.

Open Source CMS systems bring to the masses the functionality of a dynamic web site previously only the domain of companies willing to spend substantial sums of money on development and maintenance.

Appendix 1 – CSS Styles List

Below is a list of all of the currently known Joomla!-specific CSS styles. Note that this does not cover the basic styles that you would also normally configure, such as BODY, P, TD, TH, H1 etc.

#active_menu
#blockrandom
#contact_email_copy
#contact_text
#emailForm
#mod_login_password
#mod_login_remember
#mod_login_username
#poll
#search_ordering
#search_searchword
#searchphraseall
#searchphraseany
#searchphraseexact
#voteid1,#voteid2....
.adminform
.article_seperator
.back_button
.blog
.blog_more
.blogsection
.button
.buttonheading
.category
.clr
.componentheading
.contact_email
.content_rating
.content_vote
.contentdescription
.contentheading
.contentpagetitle
.contentpane
.contentpaneopen
.contenttoc

.createdate
.fase4rdf
.footer
.frontpageheader
.inputbox
.latestnews
.mainlevel
.message
.modifydate
.module
.moduletable
.mostread
.newsfeed
.newsfeeddate
.newsfeedheading
.pagenav
.pagenav_next
.pagenav_prev
.pagenavbar
.pagenavcounter
.pathway
.polls
.pollsborder
.pollstableborder
.readon
.readon:hover
.search
.searchintro
.sectionentry1
.sectionentry2
.sectionheader
.sitetitle
.small
.smalldark
.sublevel
.syndicate
.syndicate_text
.text_area
.toclink
.weblinks
.wrapper

Appendix 2 – Quick Guide to installation and configuration

Below is a bulleted guide to the general processes of installing and configuring a Joomla! powered site. This guide assumes that you are creating a brand new site and installing Joomla! to its final installation directory (rather than installing to a test folder and moving the site later). Where appropriate you will find the menu options in brackets.

- Download the latest version of Joomla! from joomla.org
- Buy your web space and domain, ensuring it supports PHP and mySQL
- Unzip and upload Joomla! to your space via your FTP software
- Run the installation wizard by typing in your URL
- Once successfully completed, delete the \installation directory using your FTP software
- Install the TMEDIT text editor
- Go into Configuration, run through each tab and modify any relevant fields/check boxes. Main items that generally require changing are offline/system error messages, content parameters, Meta tags, statistics and SEO
- Install your template(s) and make your selected template the default
- Create your sections (Content, Section Manager)
- Create your categories (Content, Category Manager)
- Install and configure your additional components, modules and mambots
- Upload any standard graphics you intend to use (Site, Media Manager)
- Configure your front page layout and item sort order (Menu, Main Menu, followed by first option in the menu)
- Start adding your content, remembering to specify which content items are to be displayed on your front page. Remember also to add Meta tags to content items
- Enable SEO (Site, Configuration, SEO) and rename htaccess.txt to .htaccess using your FTP software - test all components within the frontend of your site to ensure that everything works normally
- Perform a backup of your site

Glossary

Archive – Area allocated to content that is no longer required within your main sections and categories, but that is still required on the site.

Blog – A blog is basically a journal that is available on the web. The activity of updating a blog is "blogging" and someone who keeps a blog is a "blogger." Blogs are typically updated daily using software that allows people with little or no technical background to update and maintain the blog. In relation to Joomla!, postings on a blog are almost always arranged in chronological order with the most recent additions featured most prominently. Blog view is reference to the way in which the introduction text is displayed.

Broadband – High speed, permanent Internet connection.

CSS – Cascading Style Sheets. Used within web pages to maintain a common look and feel across all pages. Once a CSS document is created all font sizes, styles and colours are defined in one place, allowing all pages to be updated from one source. CSS can be used for much more than just text formatting.

CSV – Comma Separated Values. Standard format for importing or exporting data. Each field is separated by a comma.

FTP – File Transfer Protocol. The name used for the software that transfers files between your computer and a web server.

GIF – Graphic file format mainly used for images on web sites. Is limited to 256 colours or less – decreasing the number of colours reduces the file size, so can result in a very graphical page that can load very quickly.

ISP – Internet Service Provider. A company that provides you with access to the internet, either through dial-up or ADSL/Cable modem (broadband).

JPG – (pronounced Jay-Peg and also known as JPEG). Graphic file format mainly used for pictures on web sites due to its high compression ratios, which result in small file sizes.

Open Source – Software that is not only free, but the source code is also openly available for modification. The Linux operating system, Joomla!/Mambo CRM systems and mySQL database system are good examples of this.

Glossary

Newsgroup – An electronic discussion group allowing you to post messages that others can see and reply to, building a 'thread' of messages linked by a common subject. Newsgroups are generally free to subscribe to.

PDF – (Portable Document Format). Standard format for electronic document distribution. Developed by Adobe. A free PDF viewer is available from www.adobe.com

SEO – Search Engine Optimisation. Many web submission companies now call themselves 'SEO Experts'. Also referred to as SEM (Search Engine Marketing).

SSL – Secure Socket Layers. Any secure site (that starts with a URL of https://) is using SSL to encrypt its contents. This gives visitors to online stores confidence that their credit card details cannot be stolen.

URL – Term used for a web address. Stands for Unique Resource Location.

W3C – World Wide Web Consortium. This is the organisation behind many of the web standards, such as HTML and CSS. Their web address is www.w3.org.

WYSIWYG – What You See Is What You Get. Term used to describe applications that display on-screen what will be output to a different media e.g. printer.

Zip – a compressed file format, ideal for reducing the size of one or many files (such as graphics).

Index

Access levels, 56
　restrictions, 55
Actinic, 14
Adding content, 43
Additional functionality, 91
Add-ons, 91
Administration, 33
Archiving content, 53
Auction systems, 11
Automatic site translation, 99

Backend, 9
Backing up, 109
Banner adverts, 11

Categories, 37, 56
Classified adverts, 11, 99
CMS, 9, 13
　vs HTML, 12
CMS-powered site, 14
Community support, 11
Components, 10, 34, 92
Content, 34, 43, 46
Content meta tags, 87
Content of site, 11
Costs, 12
Creating a section, 40
Creating categories, 41
CSS, 72
　Styles 119
Custom design, 69

Database, 24
　information, 28
Directories, 27
Downloads, 12
Dreamweaver, 13, 69

E-commerce, 11
Evaluating a CMS system, 17
ExtCalendar, 99
Extensions, 100

EZ Store, 98

Forums, 11
Free Joomla templates, 64
Frequently asked questions, 98
FTP software, 23
Functionality, 98

Getting software, 22
Global meta tags, 86
Glossary, 99

Help, 35
Home, 34
.htaccess file, 79
HTML-based site, 14

Image gallery, 99
Images, 46, 48
Installation, 21
Installers, 35
Installing templates, 63
　CMS, 21
Introductory text, 45, 47
ISP, 21

Joom!fish, 101
Joomla!, 18
Joomla! templates, 69
Joomlaboard Forums, 98
JoomlaXplorer file manager, 99

Keywords, 81

L.A.M.P., 21
Link to menu, 46

Macromedia Contribute, 13
Main text, 45, 47
Making Joomla! templates, 69
Mambo, 12, 18
Mambots, 35, 92

124

Index

Media Manager, 59
Menu, 34
Messages, 35
Meta information, 46
Meta tags, 51, 85
Modifying existing template, 66
Modules, 10, 34, 92
Multi-lingual sites, 101
mySQL, 10

New folder, 60
  sites, 24

Open source software, 12
Opensourcecms.com, 17
Optimising the site, 79

Parameters, 46, 51
Pasting woes, 47
PayPal, 14
PHP files, 10
  scripting language, 10
phpMyAdmin, 109
Pre-installation check list, 26
Public backend, 56
Public frontend, 55
Publishing, 46
Publishing settings, 47

Replacing an existing site, 24

Search engine optimisation, 80
Search engines, 79
Sections, 45
Sections and categories, 37

Security, 55
  vulnerabilities, 13
SimpleFAQ, 98
Site, 34
Site map, 88
  generator, 98
Site template manager, 63
Source files, 23
Space, 21
Special user parameter, 57
Standard front page, 31
Static content, 53
Static site, 10
Structuring your content, 37
System, 35

Tabbed menu, 45
Template, 63
Templates, 10
Testing a template, 75
TinyMCE editor, 49
Title, 29, 44
  alias, 45
TMEDIT, 50
Translation, 99
Trial versions, 17

Uploading a file, 60
User registration, 57

Virtue Mart, 98
Wordtracker, 83
Wrapper, 53

XML file, 73